THE
BEAUTY
OF
COMPOUNDING

A Beginner's Guide To Investing

OYENIKE ADETOYE   ACMA, CGMA

The Beauty of Compounding

This book is designed to highlight the simple basics of investing to get you started. **"The Beauty of Compounding"** is all about financial literacy on how to best manage your money so it can exponentially grow.

OTHER BOOKS BY OYENIKE ADETOYE

❖ NonSecrets of the Financially Secure – Volume 1

❖ NonSecrets of the Financially Secure – Volume 2

❖ NonSecrets of the Financially Secure – Volume 3

❖ NonSecrets of the Financially Secure – Volume 4

❖ NonSecrets of the Financially Secure – Volume 5

❖ Praying for your Finances

❖ Financial Nakedness

❖ Financially Smart Teens & Young Adults

Dedication

This book is dedicated to my Mother:
Stella Ajoke Akintayo

You parted this world 16 years ago, but the values you have instilled in me and your legacy lives on.

Treasured in my heart you'll stay until we meet again ♡

The Beauty of Compounding

Acknowledgements

To God, who inspired the writing of this book.

To my darling husband and beautiful daughters, for cheering me on while I spent late nights and early mornings working on this book.

To my amazing siblings, for being a strong support and encouragement on this journey.

To my awesome brother Akinyemi, for editing and proofreading this book.

To everyone that has supported my dreams and inspired me to keep writing.

Thank you so much!

Oyenike.

The Beauty of Compounding

Contents

"How many millionaires do you know who have become wealthy by investing in savings accounts? I rest my case." — Robert G. Allen

The Beauty of Compounding

Reading This Book

If you ask people what's the most complicated part of managing their finances, many if not most will tell you it's investing, especially with all the recent market volatility. I have written this book to dispel some myths about investing.

This book is intended to be a broad, beginner-level resource for investors. We will be discussing the basic strategies in investment. Investing can be easy, investing can be simple, you don't need a lot of money to start investing, and investing is an important arsenal we all need on our wealth-building journey.

I have grouped this book into sections for ease of reading. **Part 1** is all about making sense of investing. The simple definition of investing and how our mindsets shape our money decisions are discussed in this section. The key differences between saving and investing are explored in this section before wrapping up by looking at myths and false beliefs about investing.

Part 2 of this book focuses on the key concepts you need to understand before venturing into investing. Compound interest, time and patience (the three catalysts of successful investing) are discussed in this section. We will conclude by delving into the must-know rules of investing.

In the **3rd part** of this book, we will discuss the steps to take in getting started with investing. We will look at the differences between active and passive investing. And conclude by exploring the different asset classes.

Part 4 of this book focuses on the different types of investing. We will explore retirement investing, stock market investing, real estate investing, and cryptocurrency investing. We will conclude this section by exploring stock trading, which is a form of investing that prioritise short-term profits over long-term gains.

Part 5 of this book deep-dive into investment strategies. We will cover Dollar-Cost Averaging, The Rule of 72, The Rule of 115 and, Diversification. We will conclude this section by discussing investing returns.

I have dedicated the last section of this book (**Part 6**) to fully explore the pitfalls and mistakes we must avoid while investing. It's easy for a beginning investor to make mistakes out of exuberance, impatience, or even ignorance. But those mistakes can be costly, making them well worth avoiding.

By the end of this book, you will have a great understanding of what investing is. Should you see something in here that you want to learn more about, I encourage you to find out more. Do some extra research, ask questions, read more books about investing and keep reading and learning every day. **KNOWLEDGE IS POWER!**

Introduction

If you are reading this, you probably understand that investing is smart and that many people have made a lot of money doing it. The problem is, you don't fully understand how to go about it, or you are scared you could lose your money, or you simply don't want to do the work involved.

The good news is, I completely relate with your concerns and worries because I was once like you. I had so many 'what if' questions on my mind about investing that I ended up not doing anything about it. Over the years, I have learnt that investing is actually not complicated. You can understand investing, and you don't even need a lot of money to get started.

I have written this book to highlight the simple basics of investing to get you started. You don't need to be scared to lose all your money if you follow basic investment rules. I want you to consider this book as your beginners' 101 cheat sheet for investing. I have taken my time to explain the basics of simple investing to inspire the proper mindset you need to succeed.

There is no better way of introducing this book than to tell the story of John and Judy. They are friends who met at the university where they both studied Economics. They graduated at the same age, 21 years old, and were both lucky to get a job with one of the FTSE 100 companies in the UK making £30,000 a year.

Judy and John both went through the typical ups and downs of life which impacted their personal finance journeys – marriage, children, travelling, unexpected job loss, career breaks, health challenges, bereavements, etc. Each retired at the age of 65.

These two buddies have many things in common, but when it comes to their personal finance and retirement planning, their approaches differ. John started saving immediately he started work by putting 10% of his earned monthly income into a savings account he specifically opened for retirement. The rate of return on this savings account was 5%. Judy too started putting money aside at the same time as John, but instead of saving, she invested her own 10% monthly income into an index mutual fund that tracks the overall market. The average long-term rate of return was 8%.

When they retire at the age of 65, John and Judy both checked the balance on their retirement accounts to see what kind of lifestyle the next 20 years will bring. John finds he has accumulated £260K. Judy's portfolio, on the other hand, has grown to a staggering £1.1M. Both figures have been adjusted for inflation and pay raise every 5-6 years.

This book will explore why such a vast difference exists between two people with similar earning and saving habits. "The Beauty of Compounding" is all about financial literacy on how to best manage your money so it can exponentially grow. While saving money is good, saving alone will not grow your wealth, you need to add investment to the game plan. From this book, you will learn about the three key ingredients required to grow your money – miracle of compound interest, time, and patience.

In case you are wondering who I am to be offering you advice about your personal finance. I am a qualified Chartered Management Accountant professional who has experienced fiscal highs and lows, been in and out of debt and has worked in various multinational FTSE 100 companies in the United Kingdom for many years. I founded LifTED Finance Consulting Ltd as a result of my personal discoveries and experiences with money on my journey to financial freedom.

Fasten your seat belt and let's get started on this road trip of multiplying your money by making your money work for you!

---------Disclaimers---------

I am not a CPA, attorney, insurance, or financial advisor, and the information in this book shall not be construed as tax, legal, insurance, or financial advice. If you need such advice, please contact a qualified CPA, attorney, insurance agent, or financial advisor.

Neither the author, nor the publisher, nor anyone involved in this book has a financial stake in any financial product mentioned in the book. Nor does anyone receive any kind of compensation from any of the products or companies mentioned.

PART 1:

MAKING SENSE OF INVESTING

1. What is Investing?

Investing can be defined as the process of putting your money to work for you. It involves using your money to buy an asset you think has a good probability of generating a safe and acceptable rate of return over time.

When done properly, investing can make more money for you than the interest you might earn in a savings account. But with reward comes risk. If an investment is done incorrectly and you make poor choices, you could lose your money.

An important secret I've learnt about personal finance and wealth-building is that you can make a lot more money a lot faster by sending your money to work for you every day, rather than just sending yourself to work every day. The true art of investing is all about letting your money work for you. It's about putting it into the right venture and letting it sit and grow over time.

You can't learn everything there is to know about investing in one day, but fortunately, you don't need to do that in order to begin your journey as a successful and profitable investor. I strongly believe anyone can reap massive financial benefits from simply taking the time to learn the basics of investing.

If you don't invest, you are missing out on opportunities to increase your financial worth. Building lasting wealth and growing your money can only happen when you invest.

In investing, risk and return are two sides of the same coin; low risk generally means low expected returns, while higher returns are usually accompanied by higher risk. But as risky as investing might sound, you will still be better off taking that leap of faith and start - your money can't grow otherwise. Not investing can cost you a lot more money than losing a little money on a bad investment.

There is virtually an infinite number of things to learn about investing. The best, most successful investors will tell you they are continually learning and constantly honing and expanding their skills!

Why You Must Invest

For a long time, I, like most people, thought that investing was "risky" and that my hard-earned money would be best kept safe if I left it in a bank. However, as I began my finance journey and started researching wealth, I realised that my money was steadily eroding in value by just sitting in cash.

Two main economic factors inherently affect the value of your money if you hold on to it and not invest it. These factors are: **interest rate** and **inflation**.

i.   Interest Rate:

Interest rates determine the amount of interest payments that savers will receive on their deposits. An increase in interest rates will make saving more attractive and should encourage saving. A cut in interest rates will reduce the rewards of saving and will tend to discourage saving.

Since the financial crisis of 2008, many financial institutions have significantly lower interest rates. The challenge low interest rate brings is that cash in the bank will only yield small returns if any at all. As at the time I am writing this book (April 2021), the Bank of England's current interest rate is 0.1%. Low interest rates significantly reduce the reward of saving.

ii. Inflation

Inflation is the second factor that affects the value of your money. This can be defined as the rate at which the prices for goods and services increase, which indirectly affects what consumers can buy for their money. To put it simply, think of inflation as the slow but steady force that makes things cost more over time.

Inflation significantly works against savers as the purchasing power of their money falls. Over time, it reduces the effective value of their savings as it cuts how far their money will go in the future.

The impact of low interest rate and inflation is more than enough reason why you must embrace investing. Despite short-term market disruptions, history shows that investing in assets such as equities, bonds and commercial properties has proved the best way to grow capital and protect it from inflation over the long-term.

2. It All Starts With Your Money Mindset

Your money mindset is your unique set of beliefs and your attitude about money. It drives the decisions you make about saving, investing, spending and handling money.

Your money mindset shapes what you believe you can and cannot do with money, how much money you believe you're allowed, entitled, and able to earn, how much you can and should spend, the way you utilise debt, how much money you give away, and your ability to invest with confidence and success.

What you believe about money, yourself, and the world shapes how your life will unfold. What's fascinating about your money mindset is that this core set of beliefs resides in your unconscious mind. And it can hang out there, dormant. But, by becoming a keen observer of your thoughts, feelings, bodily reactions, and interactions with money, you gain awareness of your current set point and the ability to change or shift your mindset.

Many of our core beliefs about money are formed in early childhood by observing and internalising the money messages we learned from our parents, friends, community, and other caregivers - especially our parents.

Growing up, my mum only saved money. Her frequent advice that I should always save for the rainy days still rings through my ears, even now that I am older. I never heard about investing from any of my circle of influences while growing up. So, I grew to only embrace saving my money, and oh was I good at it!

I was an amazing saver. The comfort and awesomeness of seeing my savings account balance increase month-on-month was so much gratifying. I knew a little about investing at the time. The scariest part of my investing knowledge was the fear that I could lose my hard-earned money because of the risk involved. So, I simply stayed clear and focused only on saving my money.

The Shift

Understanding your money mindset and where it came from helps you shift and change it. Shifting your money mindset starts with awareness. My mindset shift about investing started when I started reading more about it. I started listening to podcasts that talks more about the benefits of investing compared to just focusing on the risk elements.

Let me pause here and say this, as you become more aware of your mindset, you will encounter your own limiting beliefs and money blocks that get in the way of the shift. These beliefs prevent you from feeling and acting more abundantly. This is perfectly normal. We all have money blocks. They never go away. Limiting beliefs and money blocks keep reappearing in newer and different forms. Your work is to continually uncover the blocks, dissolve them and release them so you can build a healthier and more confident relationship with your money.

After dealing with my limiting beliefs and money blocks around the fear of investing, my perspective started to change. It was a slow but steady change that liberated my way of thinking. I started seeing investing as an opportunity to put my money where I knew it was going to return a yield of more money for me.

If you happen to be like the former me that took comfort in only saving money, here is a bit of awareness for you. Awareness that shows how much you are missing out if you only save and don't invest. Shifting your money mindset starts with awareness.

3. Saving Vs. Investing

The words "saving" and "investing" are sometimes used interchangeably, but there is a significant difference between the two. When it comes right down to it, we should be engaged in both to secure our financial future. I often tell people that saving is the starting point of investing - you cannot be a good investor if you are not a good saver. Let's look at the definition of these two terms.

Saving is the simple act of putting money aside in a safe place where it stays until you want to access it. It might earn a little interest depending on where you put it, and it will be there for you in case of an emergency or to achieve the goal you're saving for. Savings are liquid cash that is available to grab, take hold of, and deploy immediately with minimal delay. Popular savings products include savings accounts, current or checking accounts, and certificates of deposit.

Investing is taking the saving step further. It's the process of putting your money to work for you. It involves using your money to buy an asset you think has a good probability of generating a safe and acceptable rate of return over time. When done properly, it can make more money for you than the interest you might earn in a savings account. But with reward comes risk. If an investment is done incorrectly and you make poor choices, you could lose your money.

Similarities Between Saving and Investing

i. **Money accumulating strategy:** Saving and investing both share a common goal - they're both strategies that help you accumulate money.

ii. **Future benefits:** Saving and investing both involve putting money away for future reasons. When we analyse the rationale behind embarking on these financial strides, we discover we deliberately put money away for the future.

iii. **Financial planning:** Planning is an integral part of personal finance. Failing to plan ideally translates to planning to fail. The processes associated with either saving or investing involve analysis and planning of what you want, and how you will achieve what you want.

iv. **Investing is a kind of saving:** The journey towards long-term investment begins with first mastering the basics of saving. Experts argue that saving sets the blueprint or pedestal for investing. Think of savings as the building block of investment - the foundation upon which a financial house is built!

Differences Between Saving and Investing

i. **Duration:** Saving is short-term oriented while investing is long-term oriented. Generally, short-term is under 5 years and long-term is over 5 years. The duration is based on the specifics of the goal.

ii. **Risk:** A key difference between saving and investing lies in the magnitude of risk. Saving money has little risk of loss of funds and also has minimal gains. When you invest, however, you have the potential for better long-term gains or rewards, but also the potential for loss.

iii. **Interest:** The goal of investing is to make more money, while the goal of saving is to keep money safe, therefore making very little or no return. Investing helps you beat inflation through interest earned. This ensures your money's purchasing power stays strong.

iv. **Typical products:** The best type of products to put your saved money into are: secure savings accounts from reputable banks, certificate of deposits (CDs) or money market accounts. With investing, typical products include pensions, stock market investing in shares and bonds, real estate investing, and alternative investments like gold and silver.

Saving is the starting point of investing. You can only invest if you cultivate the habit of saving. Once you've mobilised an adequate sum for meeting your emergencies, you're all set to begin your journey as an investor.

Saving is the starting point of investing. A good investor should have the attributes of a good saver as well.

4. Investing Myths

In the process of writing this book, I did a lot of investigations. I was keen on finding out the reasons why people don't invest. I completely relate with the excuses some gave – for example high-interest debt payments being made, the fear of losing money, etc. But other excuses were based on myths and misconceptions about investing or a lack of knowledge about the process.

Myths are faulty belief systems learned over time. They are simply not true, and they need to be unlearned. There are tons of myths related to investing out there parading around as truth. But the real truth is that these myths are keeping people from embracing the awesomeness of investing.

I've compiled seven common investing myths below. It's about time we call out these long-believed "truths" for what they really are - MYTHS.

Myth 1: You need a lot of money:

One of the most common myths about investing is the idea that you need a lot of money to get started. Nothing could be further from the truth. If you can find £50 or $50 a month in your budget, you can and should start investing. If you think you can't squeeze that amount out of your budget, go and make it happen by cutting down your expenses and/or getting a part-time job. Now, if you carry high-interest debt or haven't set up your emergency account yet, you should attend to that first. But once you do, investing should be a priority on your list.

Myth 2: It's too risky to invest:

Of course, there are risks involved with investing. That's why it always comes with this rather abrupt warning: 'you may not get back what you invest'. But too risky to the extent of not partaking in it? I don't think so. All investments can be categorised on a scale of risk. At the extreme end of the spectrum, you've got the high-risk, these are not for the faint-hearted. At the more sedate end of the spectrum, you will find some very low-risk investments. Whatever your risk appetite, there's an investment out there to match it – from the super cautious to the highly adventurous and everything in between.

Myth 3: Investing is too complex:

When we do not understand something, it is human nature to consider it to be too complex for us to ever master and so we neglect it altogether. When faced with a new task, negative thoughts creep in like "I'm not good with money" or "I'm not smart enough to invest". These are self-limiting beliefs that can be overcome when we seek more understanding. The idea of investing may seem daunting at first, by considering your weakness to be a lack of knowledge rather than a lack of ability, you can easily break your self-imposed barriers to discover that investing is not as complex as you think it is. Warren Buffett says it nicely in one of his quotes: "Investing is simple, but not easy".

Myth 4: Investing is only for rich people:

Maybe in the past investing was perceived to be for rich people. Today, this is a myth! It's never been easier for anyone to invest, even if money is tight. Fractional shares have broken the barrier of entry that used to exist in the past. People can now invest in stocks that cost thousands of pounds/dollars for as little as a few pounds/dollars. Take, for example, US stock Berkshire Hathaway as at the time of writing this book is priced at $437,131. If you were to invest in a single share of this Warren Buffett company, you would need a capital of this exponential amount. Now, thanks to the availability of fractional shares, you can purchase such costly stocks without having to break the bank. You can simply invest the specific amount available in your budget.

Myth 5: The stock market is the only investing option:

When people think of investing, the first thing that comes to their mind is stocks and shares. However, there are other types of investments that can provide you with a little diversity - bonds, real estate, commodities, and even currencies are all choices for investing. If the stock market makes you a little nervous, there are other options.

Myth 6: Investing is too time-consuming:

Some people picture an investor as someone that constantly studies financial reports and spends hours adjusting stock screeners to get just the right stock at just the right time. But you don't need to be watching price changes daily. And you certainly don't need to be buying, selling or moving your money around in reaction to the market movements. The hands-off investor often ends up with more than the busy one. If you get involved with index investing, you might not have to do a lot of trying to find the "right" fit. Robo-advisors can help you build a portfolio based on your long-term goals and risk tolerance, without taking up more than a few minutes of your time.

Myth 7: Investing is just like gambling:

This is a common concern of many. Sure, I see some similarities. Both involve risk and choice - specifically, the risk of capital with hopes of future profit. But gambling is typically a short-lived activity while investing can last a lifetime. Also, there is a negative expected return to gamblers, on average and over the long run. On the other hand, investing typically carries with it a positive expected return on average over the long run - the odds are always in your favour.

I often ask people to tell me their **'WHY'** for investing? It is important to know the motivation behind your decision to invest your money. It's okay if you have many answers to this question, but there is a big problem if you have no answer at all. Having clear reasons or purposes for investing is critical to investing successfully.

Part 1 Recap

- Investing is the act of allocating resources, usually money, with the expectation of generating an income or profit.

- Taking the time to acquire even a very rudimentary knowledge of investing will put you well ahead of your peers in terms of financial literacy, and ultimately, in terms of financial success.

- Becoming a successful investor starts with having the right mindset. By cultivating a strong investing mindset, you can be prepared for tough investing scenarios and put yourself in better situations for financial success.

- Saving money is as important as investing money. Part of your personal finance planning is to incorporate both on our wealth-building journey. Saving complements investing.

- Investing myths are faulty belief systems learned over time. They are simply not true, and they need to be unlearned.

Saving is the starting point of investing.

PART 2:

CONCEPTS YOU SHOULD UNDERSTAND BEFORE INVESTING

The Beauty of Compounding

5.   Catalysts of Successful Investing

In the investing world, a catalyst is anything that precipitates a drastic change in the outcome of an investment. The three catalysts that positively affect the outcome of investments are: the power of compound interest, time and patience.

1.   <u>Compound Interest:</u>

Compound interest simply means earning interest on both the money you invest and the interest you earn. Think of it as the cycle of earning "interest on interest" which can cause wealth to rapidly snowball. It's because of this that your wealth can grow exponentially. I like to refer to it as your money working for you; its impact is incredibly powerful.

Albert Einstein calls it the eighth wonder of the world. Those who understand it can apply this powerful force and accelerate their wealth. Those who don't understand it will often let their debts snowball out of control, effectively paying back perpetually growing debts to their creditors.

One cool thing about compound interest is that it does not discriminate. If you're cash-rich, compound interest can make you richer by growing your wealth when you invest. And if you're bad-debt poor, compound interest can make you poorer by also growing your debt. It has no respect for age, race, gender, ethnicity or religion. Anyone in the world can earn compound interest, and its impact is huge.

Let's look at a simple example of how compound interest works. Let's say you have £100 to invest, paying 7% interest each year for ten years. At the end of the first year, you'd have £107. Then in year two, you would get 7% of £107, which is £7.49, totalling £114.49. And at the end of ten years, you'd have £196.72. Not only does the amount you invested grow each year, but the interest gained from the previous year also grows. That's why it's called compound interest.

The power of compound interest is one of the best reasons to start investing early. Because you earn interest on your interest, once you set it in motion, it takes on a life of its own - even if you never add another penny to your principal.

The table below illustrates how compounding works. If someone invests £10,000 yearly and leaves the money invested in the stock market over a period of years assuming a conservative 5% annual return, more than £100,000 profit would have accrued over 50 years of letting the money grow.

How Compounding Works

Time Invested	Amount	Return*	Total
1 year	£10,000	£500	£10,500
10 years	£10,000	£6,289	£16,289
20 years	£10,000	£16,533	£26,533
30 years	£10,000	£33,219	£43,219
40 years	£10,000	£60,400	£70,400
50 years	£10,000	£104,674	£114,674
60 years	£10,000	£176,792	£186,792

*Assumes 5% annual returns net of fees and charges

2. Time

Compound interest and time work hand in hand. In fact, the most important factor when it comes to earning compound interest is time. The more time you have, the longer you can allow your money to grow.

Have a look at the graph below. The first investor invested £50,000 and remained in the market for a 20-year period. The second investor put in exactly the same amount (£50,000), but only started investing 10 years later.

The Beauty of Compounding

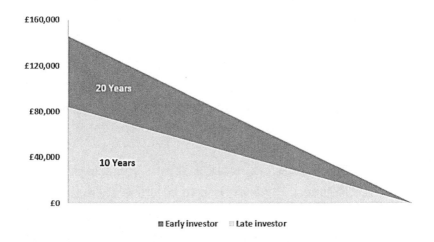

Investor	Invested Amount	Time Invested	Ending Balance
Early investor	£50,000	20 years	£145,408
Late investor	£50,000	10 years	£83,754

You can see that even though each invested the same amount of money (£50,000) at the same average return of 7%, the only thing different between these investors is the amount of time their money had to grow. There is no substitute for time when it comes to investing.

Time can be a powerful weapon to counter volatility and increase your chances of a strong return. The longer you leave your money to grow, the larger your account balance becomes. Your success with investing will come from the time in the market, not timing the market.

3. <u>Patience</u>

Patience is the third catalyst that makes investing works. It works hand in hand with the other two catalysts - compound interest and time. Compound interest will not make you a millionaire overnight; building wealth takes time, patience and consistent contribution.

Successful investors develop several valuable skills over their lifetimes. Patience is one of those skills that need developing. We're not born patient. In fact, lack of patience is one of the reasons many people don't invest. But patience can be learned and, if you are an investor, learning it could help you reach your financial goals.

Patience often involves staying calm in situations where you lack control. To be patient is to endure some short-term hardship for a future reward. Impatient investors let anxiety and emotion rule their decision-making; this could significantly damage their long-term returns. Wealth requires time to develop; patience is key!

This quote by Charlie Munger sums things perfectly: "Waiting helps you as an investor and a lot of people just can't stand to wait. If you didn't get the deferred-gratification gene, you've got to work very hard to overcome that."

Patience and investing are
natural partners.

6. Rules of Investing

Investing allows you to significantly grow your money over time thanks to the power of compounding. While this sounds fantastic, it is important to note that you can't begin to work out how much money you can afford to put aside for investments if you are not in full control of your finances.

You shouldn't think about investing money if doing so means risking a roof over your head or default in the payment of essential bills and other necessities. I have highlighted a few golden rules you must know before venturing into investing. Make sure you seek professional investment advice for more clarity before you embark on your investing journey.

Rule 1: Know your investment goal:

What is your 'WHY' for investing? What do you want to invest in? Are you investing for retirement, or to earn an income, or to pay for your children's education, or to grow your fortune? Having a clear purpose for investing and knowing exactly what to invest in is critical to investing successfully.

Rule 2: You need money to invest:

Investing is the act of allocating money with the expectation of generating an income or profit. You need money to invest, so you having an income is a must (preferably a steady income). It is recommended that one should consistently invest over time to enjoy the full benefit of compounding and the Dollar-Cost Averaging (DCA) strategy. We will discuss DCA in more details in Chapter 15.

You shouldn't think about investing money if doing so means risking a roof over your head or default in the payment of essential bills and other necessities.

Rule 3: You have a solid emergency fund:

Smart investors must have an emergency fund in place to cover an emergency like sudden unemployment. You must be able to weather a storm when life happens. Ideally, you should have 3 to 6 months of your basic living expenses put aside before you start putting money aside for investing. Emergency fund takes priority over investing.

Rule 4: You have paid off your high-interest debt?

This is a very important question to ask yourself because in the long run, the money you'll be throwing away in interest payments to your high-interest debt is higher than any returns you will earn from your investments. Focus on paying down your debt before venturing into investing. One works for you, the other works against you. Focus on getting rid of the one that could drag you down - your high-interest debts.

Rule 5: Don't invest money you'll need right away:

Investing is for long-term e.g. 8 years or more. Some investments require you to tie up money for months or years to earn returns and withdrawing early can trigger penalties. If you're going to need cash right away (say, to pay next month's mortgage or next year's college tuition), you don't want to risk not being able to access money when you need it. A good rule of thumb is to keep cash in a savings account if you'll need it within the next two years, rather than investing it.

Rule 6: You've done your due diligence and research:

Throwing your money haphazardly into investments you don't understand is a sure way to lose it quickly. Never invest in something you don't understand. Taking calculated risks require that you understand both the potential reward and the likelihood of loss. To avoid big losses, take the time to research the fundamentals of what, where and how you are investing your money.

Rule 7: Invest early and invest as much as you can:

One important investing strategy is to start sooner and stay invested longer. This allows compounding to flex its muscle. Compound interest works magic on your money, turning small and steady investments into a big nest egg that buys financial freedom. The sooner you start investing in assets that produce a reasonable rate of return, and the more you invest in those assets, the harder your money will work for you.

Rule 8: Know your risk tolerance:

How much risk you can tolerate? What will make you sleep at night? Are you an aggressive investor or a conservative investor? Higher risk is associated with a greater probability of higher return and lower risk with a greater probability of smaller return. The general rule of thumb is to invest in riskier assets (e.g. stocks) when you are young and have time to recover from downturns. As you get older, move some of your invested money to safer investments (e.g. bonds) with a lower potential rate of return, but less chance of losing it all.

Rule 9: Have realistic expectations on performance:

A realistic expectation of how your investments will perform is important. E.g. average return of the stock market investment since inception (1817) has been 8%. This is the average, meaning you will not experience this every single year. In a bull market (a time when the price of stocks is rising), you could see returns of 15% per year or more. And in a bear market (a time when the price of stocks is falling), you could see a 20% loss or more. Despite the peaks, valleys, over the long-term 8% return has stayed consistent.

Rule 10: Diversify your portfolio:

Don't put all your eggs in one basket. Try to diversify as much as you can to lower your risk exposure. To reduce the likelihood of big losses, spread your money around a mix of different asset classes. If you spread your investments across lots of different industries (e.g. pharmaceuticals, technology), in lots of different countries, you can protect yourself against the ups and downs of any one part of your portfolio.

Rule 11: Don't miss out on Employer's "free money":

In many employer-sponsored retirement plans, the employer will match some or all of your contributions. If your employer offers a retirement plan and you do not contribute enough to get your employer's maximum match, you are passing up "free money" for your retirement savings. Don't be one of those people that wait until their friends start retiring to start investing. The sooner you start investing, the earlier retirement will become an option for you.

Rule 12: Keep costs low:

Investment costs are unrecoverable; every penny paid in management fees, taxes, transaction fees, and trading expenses is money out of your pocket. Investment costs might not seem like a big deal, but they add up, compounding along with your investment returns. In other words, you don't just lose the tiny amount of fees you pay, you also lose all the growth that money might have had for years into the future. Costs are one of the driving factors that dictate whether you'll reach your goal, and they're one of the many factors completely within your control. So, give them the time and attention they deserve.

Rule 13: Don't panic:

Investments can go down as well as up. Don't be tempted to sell funds just because everyone else is. Emotion is the enemy of smart investing. Do not let emotions like fear and anxiety cause you to make the rash decision to sell into a falling market. Many want to invest and get quick cash. But thinking this way commonly leads to making wrong, poor investments.

To get the best returns from your investments, you must be prepared to think long-term.

Part 2 Recap

- The three catalysts that positively affect the outcome of investments are: the power of compound interest, time and patience.

- Compound interest refers to the principle of earning interest on both the money you invest and the interest you earn. Think of it as the cycle of earning "interest on interest" which can cause wealth to rapidly snowball.

- Your success with investing will come from the time in the market, not timing the market. Time can be a powerful weapon to counter volatility and increase your chances of a strong return.

- Successful investors develop several valuable skills over their lifetimes. Patience is one of those skills that need developing.

- You shouldn't think about investing money if doing so means risking a roof over your head or default in the payment of essential bills and other necessities. There are few golden rules you must know before venturing into investing.

The Beauty of Compounding

PART 3:

GETTING STARTED WITH INVESTING

The Beauty of Compounding

7. Preparing to Invest

One of the best financial decisions you can make for yourself is to start investing. In fact, anyone that is not investing is missing out tremendously. And the good news is that you don't need to be a financial professional, or have a PhD in finance, or read the finance section of the newspapers to make a start. I've listed out a few things you need to know so you can be adequately prepared before embarking on this awesome journey of investing.

i. Educate yourself:

As Benjamin Franklin rightly put it: "An investment in knowledge pays the best interest." When it comes to investing, nothing will pay off more than educating yourself. Knowledge is an essential asset when you're investing; knowledge is power. The most important thing you can do to be a successful investor is to learn, learn, learn and never stop learning.

Investing isn't complicated if you're willing to spend the time to learn about it. Read books about investing, listen to podcasts on investing, attend seminars and workshops where they talk about investing, have an open mind and ask questions from successful investors. You only know what you know, be willing to learn, be willing to unlearn, and be willing to relearn.

ii. **Have a plan and set investing goals:**

Planning and setting goals are crucial when you want to embark on your investing journey.

The planning stage is when you honestly answer questions like: How much can I afford to invest each month? How long will it take to reach my investing goal? How much risk can I take? What types of investments should I consider? Answering these questions can take some time, but the answers are invaluable for your planning.

Understanding the motivation behind your decision to invest that spare cash is critical to stay 'committed to the cause' and to avoid straying off course in times of uncertainty. After learning about the different types of investments and how they work, set target dates and financial goals for your assets. Setting investing goals for yourself allows you to overpower fear with determination and grit. Setting target dates for yourself will lay out a timeline for your financial journey.

iii. **Stick to a simple investment strategy**

The simpler your investment strategy, the better. Stick your retirement savings in a target-date retirement fund. Come up with a very simple portfolio spread across two or three different asset classes, and just stick to it as a start.

Complicated investment strategies often require much more work and stress than more straightforward ones do, and often for no more profit. A simple investment approach prevents you from becoming overwhelmed and keeps you on track.

iv. **Start small, keep contributing and watch your money grow:**

The reason many people don't invest is that they feel they don't have enough money to invest. There's a misconception that you need lots of money to become an investor, but nothing could be farther from the truth, especially today. Lots of barriers to entry have been removed and you can start investing with as little as £10 or $10.

Don't be afraid to start small. Begin with sums of money that you can afford to lose and not risk too much while learning. As you watch your balance grow, you'll become more comfortable investing more considerable sums if you can afford to. Compound interest is the primary principle behind investing. More money in your account means more interest is compounded.

v. **Ride out the highs and the lows:**

More often than not, things don't always go as planned. Stocks are going to go up and down. Bonds are going to go up and down. Real estate is going to go up and down. Don't be discouraged. Always remember you are in this investing gig for the long haul.

Stock prices rise and fall, economies expand and contract, and investors with risky plans panic. Making a panicked move based on a short-term drop or a short-term jump is probably going to put you in a worse long-term position, especially when you add in transaction fees and taxes (if applicable). Start small, learn along the way, diversify your portfolio, and exercise lots and lots of patience. Patience is a virtue you need when investing!

Setting investing goals for yourself allows you to overpower fear with determination and grit.

8. Active and Passive Investing

There are two broad categories of investing styles: active and passive investing.

1. Active Investing:

Active investing is an investing style that involves ongoing buying and selling activities. Active investors purchase investments and continuously monitor their activity to exploit profitable conditions.

Active investors often use quantitative and technical analyses, including ratio analysis, stock chart analysis and other mathematical measures to determine whether to buy or sell. The investment horizon can be months, days or even hours or minutes. Active investors look at the price movements of the investment many times a day with the motive of seeking short-term profits.

You will not be surprised to learn that active investing requires someone to act in the role of Portfolio or Active Money Manager. The goal of this investment expert is to beat the stock market's average returns and be able to immediately take advantage of short-term price fluctuations.

So, while the active money manager will argue they will perform better in a rising market, they also argue that they will lose less in a falling market.

Benefits of Active Investing

i. **Short-term opportunities:** Investors can use active investing to take advantage of short-term trading opportunities - an opportunity to perhaps outperform the market. The potential for higher returns within a short period of time is the main allure of active investing.

ii. **Flexibility:** Active Money Managers generally can invest more freely than their passive counterparts as they're not tied to any index. This means that a particular client's ethical or other requirements can be accommodated.

iii. **Risk Management:** Active investing allows Money Managers to adjust investors' portfolios to align with prevailing market conditions. For example, they can minimise potential losses by avoiding certain sectors, regions, etc. in order to reduce their clients' risks in the market.

iv. **Tax Management:** Active Money Managers can tailor tax management strategies to individual investors. E.g. by selling investments that are losing money to offset the taxes on the big winners.

Drawbacks of Active Investing

i. **Performance is dependent on the skill of the Manager:** Without a skilled and talented Active Money Manager, there is a risk of investing in an actively managed fund that underperforms. Active Managers are free to buy any investment they think would bring high returns, which is great when the analysts are right but terrible when they're wrong.

ii. **Takes a significant amount of time:** Active investing takes time. Much of this time is spent researching the market, combing through dense financial reports to learn more about specific securities, and then acting on that information.

iii. **Higher costs:** Active investing can be costly due to the potential for numerous transaction costs and high active management fees. Payment is made for the expertise and resources required for Active Managers regardless of how successfully the fund performs. All those fees and costs over decades of investing can kill returns.

iv. **Minimum investment amounts:** Many active funds and investments often set minimum investment thresholds for prospective investors. For example, a hedge fund might require new investors to make a starting investment of £200,000.

2. Passive Investing

Passive investing is an investing style that maximises returns by minimising buying and selling. Most people graduate from pre-investor status and enter the investment world through the window of passive investing. It's the most common starting point for beginner investors.

The passive investor type usually employs all the basics of sound personal financial planning - own your own home, fund tax-deferred retirement plans, asset allocation, save at least 10% of earnings, etc. If you follow these foundational principles and begin early enough in life, then passive investing is likely all you will ever need to attain financial independence.

The defining characteristic of passive investment strategies is their simplicity. They require less knowledge and skill in making them accessible to the general populace. "Buy and hold" with mutual funds or stocks, fixed asset allocation, averaging down, and buying real estate at retail prices are examples of passive investment strategies.

Benefits of Passive Investing

i. **An excellent way to achieve diversification:** Maintaining a well-diversified portfolio is important to successful investing, and passive investing allows that to happen.

ii. **You are in charge of your portfolio choices:** No portfolio managers interference. You tend to have a clear and thorough understanding of what you are investing in.

iii. **Low cost, fees and operating expenses:** There is nobody picking stocks, so oversight is much less expensive. Management fees are usually lower than actively managed investing.

iv. **Simple, quick and easy access to the market:** Passive investing can offer a quick and easy way to gain access to the stock market. Investing and owning an index or a group of indices is a lot easier to implement when compared to any dynamic strategy which requires constant research and planning.

Drawback of Passive Investing:

i. **Lack of control over financial security:** Because it is passive, it lacks many risk control strategies and overlooks the value-added opportunities available only to those with greater skills.

ii. **No chance of outperformance:** As a passive investor, you tend to endure higher volatility and possibly lower returns when compared to the successful execution of an active investment strategy. By definition, passive funds can never beat the markets, even during times of turmoil, as their core holdings are locked in to track the market.

iii. **Very limited:** Passive investing is somehow limited to a specific index or predetermined set of investments with little to no variance. Investors are therefore locked into those holdings, no matter what happens in the market.

Active Vs. Passive: Which is better?

Choosing between a passive and active fund involves many factors, but in recent years, investors have shown a surprising preference for one over the other. Many seem in favour of the passive investing strategy because of their low fees and their stellar performance.

While passive investing has grown in popularity over the last few years, active management however has the ability to help investors improve their risk-adjusted returns. Active managers can be especially helpful during periods of market stress when outperformance can be most critical for investors.

The most favourable result may come from combining both strategies – active and passive. I strongly believe there is room for both. Active and passive investing can co-exist and investors can benefit from both worlds by leveraging the valuable attributes of each. Market conditions change all the time, so it often takes an informed eye to decide when and how much to shift toward passive as opposed to active investments.

Some investors have very strong opinions about the "best of both worlds" approach. If your top priority as an investor is to reduce your fees and trading costs, an all-passive portfolio might make sense for you. But if you are an investor that cares more about factors like risk, return and liquidity than fees, a mixed approach may be beneficial for you.

Choosing one (or both) strategy requires a careful assessment of risks, opportunities and objectives for everyone involved. Each person is unique and many choose an appropriate strategy style as their skills, experience, and portfolio grow. There is therefore no single "right" answer to which investment strategy is better, it all boils down to personal preference.

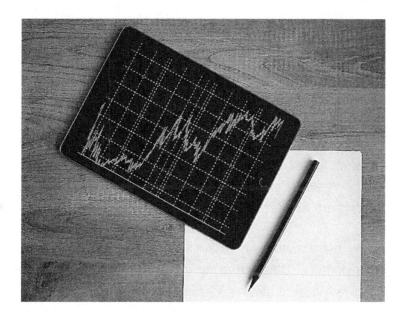

Active and passive investing can co-exist and investors can benefit from both worlds by leveraging the valuable attributes of each.

9. Asset Classes

There is an endless list of specific investments you can make, but nearly all investments fall into one or the other of a handful of categories commonly referred to as "asset classes".

Asset classes are defined as groups of investments that have similar characteristics, behave in a similar way, and are subject to the same laws and regulations. When dealing with investments, it is essential to understand the different asset classes and which investments fall into each. Asset classes are the raw ingredients of an investment portfolio.

Many investors focus on asset classes as a way to diversify their portfolio. Different asset classes have different cash flows streams and varying degrees of risk. Investing in several asset classes ensures a certain amount of diversity in investment selections.

There are four broad classes of assets:
 i. Equities (stocks)
 ii. Fixed income (bonds)
 iii. Cash and cash equivalents
 iv. Real estate and tangible assets

If your portfolio includes investments spread across these four asset classes, it is considered balanced - which is ideal because it helps to reduce risk while maximising return.

Let's deep dive into the different asset classes.

i. **Equities:** These are also referred to as stocks. Equity represents ownership. When you purchase shares in a company, you're purchasing ownership in that company and you become a shareholder.

Equity investors have an expectation that the shares purchased will rise in value in the form of capital gains and/or generate capital dividends. Neither of these is guaranteed and there is always the risk that the share price will fall below the level at which you invested.

ii. **Fixed income:** These are also referred to as bonds. Bonds are a form of loan agreement traded between owners (i.e. bondholders). Corporate bonds are issued by companies, and government bonds are issued by the central government. There are also municipal bonds, which are issued by local authorities, but these are uncommon.

Bonds provide a regular stream of dividend payments to investors until their maturity date. At maturity, investors are repaid the principal amount they had invested. Bonds are perceived to be lower risk than equities. They, however, deliver lower returns over the long-term.

iii. **Cash and cash equivalents:** These include money in the form of currencies (local and foreign), physical bills, treasury bills, coins and any money market liquid investments and certificate of deposits that can readily be converted into cash within 3 months or less.

In comparison to bonds and equities, these are considered to have lower risk, but also have lower returns. They can be a useful tool for very risk-averse investors or as a temporary home for money in between longer-term decisions.

iv. **Real estate and tangible assets:** These are assets you can physically see and touch. Real estate is the most common type of tangible assets that people own, but commodities like gold, silver, copper and livestock, also fall into this category.

These types of assets offer protection against inflation. Their tangible nature leads to them being considered more of a "real" asset because they differ from assets that exist only in the form of financial instruments, such as derivatives. Tangible assets are less affected by shifts in currency values and other macroeconomic factors that greatly impact other financial assets.

With some investments, you can leave the asset allocation decision to experts. These are called **automatic asset allocation**. For example, in pension or retirement investing, if you do not say how you want your contributions invested, your money will automatically go into a default fund. Generally, this will be some sort of 'lifestyle' fund, where the proportion invested in shares will be high if you're young and will automatically shift to the safer asset classes of cash and bonds as your retirement date approaches. We will discuss retirement investing in more details in Chapter 10.

You can hedge your investments in one asset class and reduce your risk exposure by simultaneously holding investments in other asset classes. The practice of reducing investment portfolio risk by diversifying your investments across different asset classes is referred to as asset allocation. We will discuss diversification in more details in Chapter 18.

"If your portfolio includes investments spread across the four asset classes, it is considered balanced - which is ideal because it helps to reduce risk while maximising return."

Part 3 Recap

- Preparation is key before you venture into investing. Education, having a plan, setting investing goals, sticking to a simple investment strategy, starting small while consistently contributing, and exercising lots of patience while riding out the highs and the lows of investing are some of the suggested preparation steps.

- Active investing is an investing style that involves ongoing buying and selling activity by the investor. Active investors purchase investments and continuously monitor their activity to exploit profitable conditions

- Passive investing is an investing style that maximises returns by minimising buying and selling. Most people graduate from pre-investor status and enter the investment world through the window of passive investing. It is the most common starting point for beginner investors.

- Asset classes are groups of investments that have similar characteristics, behave in a similar way, and are subject to the same laws and regulations. There are four broad classes of assets: Equities (stocks), Fixed income (bonds), Cash and cash equivalents, and Real estate and tangible assets.

- Many investors focus on asset class as a way to diversify their portfolio. Different asset classes have different cash flows streams and varying degrees of risk. Investing in several asset classes ensures a certain amount of diversity in investment selections.

PART 4:

TYPES OF INVESTING

The Beauty of Compounding

10. Retirement Investing

Retirement investing is all about retirement planning. It refers to the financial strategies of saving, investing, and ultimately the distribution of money meant to sustain one's self after paid work ends, i.e. during retirement. Retirement investing is a long-term personal finance goal that must not be ignored.

If you've ever heard me speak in any of my events, you would have noticed that the subject of retirement is something I am very passionate about. The reason I am particular about retirement is that many people simply don't prioritise it. They also tend to ignore it until later years.

You will hear people say retirement is still decades away. Some will tell you they don't have money to save towards retirement. Some will even tell you that the government would take care of them. A recent chat I had with someone in his early 50s was shocking and very concerning. He literarily said he and his wife have no game plan for retirement. He said they just never think long-term, they always live in the moment.

I've seen so much happen to people in their old age when their body and strength are no longer as active as it was in their youthful age. Many seemingly old men and women can't stop working even after passing the retirement age because they still have tons of bills to pay monthly. They are still working not by choice, but because of necessity.

I have seen cases where many elderly struggles daily to keep a roof over their head and have a hot meal to eat. I've seen many parents become financial burdens to their children in their old age, simply because they never prioritised retirement planning during their earning years. I will never stop educating people that one of the best gifts' parents can give their children is the gift of letting those children not worry about their finances when they are old.

But on the flip side, I have also seen some people splash their wealth after retiring to help, bless, and support their children's children. This category of people has planned for their retirement during their earning days, saved and invested a significant amount of money to live independently when they are old. These people have built a sizeable nest egg in readiness for the evening season of their life; they simply have no financial need. No wonder they are enjoying peace of mind, calmness and no money worries after retiring.

Retirement is wonderful if you have two essentials: much to live on and much to live for. Retirement is not an age; it is a financial number. What it takes to retire is a solid grasp of your budget, a carefully considered investment and spending plan for your life savings, debt that's under control, and a plan you're excited about when you quit the workforce. Are you planning for your retirement?

How Retirement Investing Works

Saving money to fund a comfortable retirement is perhaps one of the biggest reasons most people invest. As such, finding the right balance between risk and return is key to a successful retirement investing strategy.

We talked about the three catalysts of successful investing in chapter 5 of this book - compound interest, time and patience. These three magic words are still the secret of successful retirement investing. Let's look at the story of these three investors - Jessica, Godwin and Abi.

Jessica saved £1,000 per month into her retirement investment account from the time she turned 25 until she turned 35. She then stopped saving but left her money in her investment account where it continued to accrue at a 7% rate until she retired at age 65.

Godwin held off and didn't start saving until age 35. Like Jessica, he also put away £1,000 per month from his 35th birthday until he turned 45. Godwin left the balance in his investment account, where it continued to accrue at a rate of 7% until age 65.

Abi didn't get around to investing until age 45. She too invested £1,000 per month for 11 years, halting her savings after her 55th birthday. She then left her money to accrue at a 7% rate until her 65th birthday.

Jessica, Godwin and Abi each saved the same amount - £132,000, over the same length of time (11 years each). The only difference was their investing starting dates. The length of time they each had to put their money to work for them and the power of compound interest over the investing period shows their different ending balances. See the summary of their investing journey below:

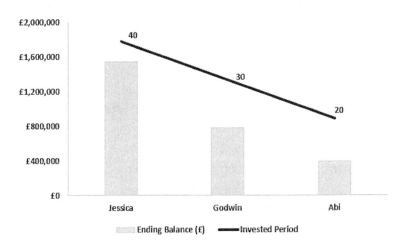

Investor	Invested Amount	Invested Period	Ending Balance
Jessica	£132,000	40 years	£1,542,710
Godwin	£132,000	30 years	£784,236
Abi	£132,000	20 years	£398,666

Thanks to the power of compound interest and time. These two powerful variables are the magic that allows investment earnings to earn interest of its own. Compound interest favours those that start investing early!

Abi can never catch up with Jessica, even if she saves for an additional 10 years.

You cannot invest for the future in the future, you can only invest for the future now while you are still earning.

Retirement Planning

Retirement planning is a multistep process that evolves over time. To have a comfortable retirement, you need to build a financial cushion that will not run out when retirement comes. Here are a few questions to consider when planning your retirement.

i.   What are your retirement goals?

ii.   What are your retirement spending needs?

iii.   How old are you and how long do you have to meet your retirement goals?

iv.   How much risk are you willing to take to meet your goals?

v.   How can you save and invest to get to your retirement goals?

vi.   What are your retirement investment options?

Your answers to these questions will determine the types of retirement accounts that can help you raise the money to fund your future.

One of the most challenging aspects of creating a comprehensive retirement plan is striking a balance between realistic return expectations and a desired standard of living. The best solution is to focus on creating a flexible investment portfolio that can be updated regularly to reflect changing market conditions and retirement objectives.

Young people that have 30-plus years until retirement can have most of their assets in riskier investments, such as stocks. Though there will be volatility, stocks have historically outperformed other securities, such as bonds, over long time periods.

Retirement Investment Options

You can save for retirement in various tax-advantaged and taxable accounts. Some are offered by your employer, while others are available through a brokerage firm or bank.

Keep in mind that retirement plan accounts are not investments themselves. Instead, they are portfolios that hold the investments. The investments would be in a variety of asset classes including private equity, real estate, infrastructure, and securities like gold that can hedge inflation. Let's deep dive into the various retirement investment options available.

i. **Defined-Benefit Pension Plan:** Also known as DB Pension Plan, this is a retirement plan that requires an employer to make contributions to a pool of funds set aside for a worker's future benefit. The pool of fund is invested on the employee's behalf, and the earnings on the investments generate income to the worker upon retirement.

The employer funds the pension plan by contributing a regular amount, usually a percentage of the employee's pay, into a tax-deferred account. Since the employer is responsible for making investment decisions and managing the plan's investments, the employer assumes all the investment and planning risks.

In this pension scheme, the income an employee will receive on retiring is based on three factors: the number of years the employee has been with that employer, the employees' pensionable earnings, and the employee's accrual rate i.e. the proportion of the earnings employee will get for each year spent in the scheme.

Pension fund assets need to be prudently managed to ensure that retirees receive promised retirement benefits. Upon retirement, the plan may pay monthly payments throughout the employee's lifetime or as a lump-sum payment. DB pension plans are often provided by the public sector e.g. NHS, Police, etc.

ii. Defined-Contribution Pension Plan:

Defined contribution pensions, also known as DC pension, can be either workplace pensions arranged by your employer, where both you and your employer contribute to the plan, or personal pensions which you arrange yourself and pay into separately from any employer.

With a workplace pension plan, employees contribute a fixed amount or a percentage of their paychecks to an account that is intended to fund their retirements. The employer will then, at times, match a portion of employee contributions as an added benefit. If an employer offers matching on your contributions, it is generally advisable to contribute the maximum amount they will match, as this is essentially free money that will grow over time and will benefit you in retirement.

Most self-employed people use a personal pension for their pension savings. With a personal pension, you choose where you want your contributions to be invested from a range of funds offered by the provider. The provider will claim tax relief at the basic rate of tax on your behalf and add it to your pension savings.

The value of a DC pension plan is based on money contributed to the scheme. Contributions are invested by the pension provider, and the performance of the fund can go down as well as up depending on how the underlying investments perform. The size of your pension pot will depend on how much your employer and/or you contribute, how long you save for, and any charges deducted by the pension provider.

Company pension plans and the USA 401(k) and 403(b) are popular defined-contribution plans commonly used by companies and organizations to encourage their employees to save for retirement.

iii. **Retirement Individual Savings Account (ISA):**

The Stock and Shares ISA and the Lifetime ISA are tax-efficient ways to save for retirement in the United Kingdom. This means you don't have to pay income tax or capital gains tax on the money you earn from your investments made through the ISA, up to a certain limit (currently £20,000 in 2021/22 tax year). Retirement ISA accounts allow you to invest in a wide range of shares, funds, investment trusts and bonds.

Lifetime ISA (LISA) allows you to build up a long-term fund for retirement or for buying your first home. You can pay in up to £4,000 a year, and the government will contribute 25% of what you've paid into the account too. That means you could get a chunky £1,000 of free cash annually.

You won't be able to take money out of the LISA account until you reach 60 years old without paying a 25% charge (unless it's for your first home). You also must be over 18 and under 40 to open a LISA investment account. Once you turn 50, you won't be able to make any more payments in, and therefore you also won't get the 25% bonus, but your savings will still earn interest.

Roth IRA is the USA's closest equivalent of the UK Stock and Shares ISA. It is an individual retirement account that provides tax-free growth and withdrawals. And similar to the UK stock and shares ISA, it has a contribution limit and threshold.

If you are unsure which retirement investment scheme to choose, it would be worth consulting a regulated financial adviser who will make a recommendation for you, based on your specific needs and circumstances. The benefit of taking regulated financial advice is you're protected if the product you buy turns out to be unsuitable or in the unlikely event the provider goes bust. Also, a financial adviser can search the entire market for you and make a recommendation that is tailored to your personal need.

How much do I need to retire?

One popular question I'm often asked is: 'How much will I need in retirement?' Many people overestimate how much they'll need to live on in retirement, thinking that they'll spend the equivalent of their wages. Experts, however, suggest you'll need between half and two-thirds of the salary you earned before retirement to maintain your lifestyle. But the truth is this; how much income you'll need in retirement is hard to know, and tricky to plan.

One thing is for sure, it's much better when you are over-prepared than when you are under-prepared. The three common rule of thumb discussed below provides a form of guidance on how much you should save and invest towards your retirement.

i.   **The Multiply by 25 Rule:** This rule estimates how much money you'll need in retirement by multiplying your desired annual income by 25. E.g. if you want to withdraw £40,000 per year from your retirement portfolio, you need £1 million in your retirement portfolio (£40,000 x 25 = £1 million.) To withdraw £50,000 per year, you need £1.25 million.

ii. **The Multiply by 33 Rule:** Some experts say the Multiply by 25 rule is a bit risky as it doesn't factor 'real' return after inflation. So, for a more conservative approach, many opt for the Multiply by 33 rule. This rule estimates how much money you'll need in retirement by multiplying your desired annual income by 33. E.g. if you want to withdraw £50,000 per year from your retirement portfolio, you need £1.65 million in your retirement portfolio (£50,000 x 33 = £1.65 million.)

iii. **The 80% Rule:** This rule suggests you'll need about 80% of your pre-retirement income to sustain your standard of living in retirement. E.g. if you make £100,000 a year now, you'll need about £80,000 per annum after you retire. This reduced figure accounts for certain expenses you probably won't have to pay anymore e.g. cost of commuting.

The above three rules are guides. By using these methods, you can get a good idea of how much you'll need to save to retire comfortably. Keep in mind that this isn't designed to be a perfect method, but a starting point to help you assess where you are, and what adjustments you might need to make to get yourself to where you need to be.

A successful retirement depends largely not only on your ability to save and invest wisely but also on your ability to plan. Just getting by isn't a good way to start decades of unemployment, diminishing employability and diminishing health. Are you on track with your long-term financial goal of a "good retirement plan" in place?

A future without a retirement plan is a scary one. It's never too late to start saving and investing for retirement!

The Beauty of Compounding

11. Stock Market Investing

The stock market is a place where buyers and sellers meet to sell shares – each one a tiny part of a company listed on an exchange. In return for your cash, a business offers you a share in its future, i.e. you own a tiny slice of that company and become a 'shareholder'.

The financial activities within a stock market are conducted through institutionalised formal exchanges or over-the-counter (OTC) marketplaces that operate under a defined set of regulations. The stock market is one of the most vital components of a free-market economy. It allows companies to raise money by offering stock shares and corporate bonds.

The stock market also allows common investors to participate in the financial achievements of the companies, make profits through capital gains, and earn money through dividends, although losses are also possible. In the long-term, the stock market helps in capital formation and economic growth for the country. The first stock market in the world was the London stock exchange. Other popular stock markets around the world include NYSE, Nasdaq, Hong Kong Exchanges, Saudi Stock Exchange, etc.

There are three common ways to invest in the stock market. You could invest in individual stocks, stock options, or stock market index.

i. Individual Stocks:

Stocks are "shares" of ownership in a particular company. When you purchase an individual company's stock, you become a partial owner of that company. That means when the company makes money, so do you. And when the company grows in value, the value of your stock grows as well.

When the price of a company's stock goes up, the value of the owner's investment in that company also goes up. The owner can then choose to sell the stock for a profit. However, when the price of a company's stock goes down, the value of the owner's investment also goes down.

ii. Stock Options:

When you purchase an option in a company, you are betting that the price of that company's stock will go up or down. Purchasing an option gives you the option to buy or sell shares of that company at a set price within a set timeframe without actually owning the stock.

Options are incredibly risky. As with most high-risk investments, there is potential for high returns, however, there is also the potential for great loss, especially if you don't know what you're doing. I don't recommend investing in options for beginners.

iii. Stock Market Index

This is an index that measures a stock market, or a subset of the stock market, that helps investors compare current price levels with past prices to calculate market performance. Investors can invest in a stock market index by buying an index fund.

An index fund is a pool or collection of different stocks designed to replicate an underlying benchmark. This benchmark could be the S&P 500, foreign telecommunication companies, or even the entire global stock market. Index fund is structured as either a mutual fund or an exchange-traded fund. It's designed to replicate the performance of the underlying benchmark as closely as possible.

Investing in the stock market is an excellent way to grow wealth. For long-term investors, stocks are a good investment even during periods of market volatility.

As a long-term investor, you need to understand that the market is a pendulum, and it is forever swinging between unjustified pessimism and unsustainable optimism.

Getting Started With Stock Market Investing

Here is how to invest in the stock market in five quick steps:

1. How do you want to invest?
2. Choose an investing account.
3. Stock investing or fund investing?
4. Determine how much to invest.
5. Optimise your investment portfolio.

Step 1: How do you want to invest?

There are three ways of going about the question of how to invest. You can hire a financial professional to manage the process for you, you can use a robo-advisor, or you can choose your stocks investments yourself. Let's look at the three options.

i. **Hiring a Financial or Investment Advisor:** A financial or investment advisor is a professional who is paid to provide investment advice and management to their clients at a flat fee or percentage of the assets they manage.

Financial advisors provide expert management of their client's portfolio, consider their goals and cash needs, help them navigate complex financial situations, answer investing questions as they come up, and provide them with continuous comprehensive financial planning.

All these services however come at a cost. Financial and investment advisors charge a fee, which varies but 1% is a good estimate. And while most are ethical and skilled at what they do, you run the risk of hiring a substandard advisor. I always recommend that if you do hire a professional to manage your finances, make sure they are fiduciary financial or investment advisor.

A fiduciary duty is the highest standard of care. It entails the hired professional is always acting in your best interest, with undivided loyalty and utmost good faith. A fiduciary financial advisor cannot recommend an investment that doesn't benefit you.

Investors with fiduciary financial advisors will therefore enjoy peace of mind when it comes to their investments. They have no worries, knowing fully well that a trustworthy professional is monitoring their asset allocations, providing guidance on their overall investment strategy, and rebalancing their investment portfolio for them.

ii. **Robo-advisor:** A robo-advisor is a brokerage that automates key components of investment planning. It works by asking a few simple questions to determine your goal and risk tolerance and then investing your money in a highly diversified low-cost portfolio of stocks and bonds. Robo-advisors then use algorithms to continuously rebalance your portfolio.

Many people who know the basics of investing don't want to spend their time researching and managing investments. Robo-advisors can allow you to put your investments on auto-pilot. Not only can a robo-advisor select your investments, but they also optimise your tax efficiency and make changes over time automatically.

Robo-advisors are known for having lower fees than their human counterparts, but it's still important to know there are associated fees for using this service. Most robo-advisors charge management fees and investment expenses.

It's important to consider the combination of these fee types, often referred to as the "all-in" cost of a robo-advisor. All-in costs typically range from 0.03% to 0.50%, but even at the higher end, this compares favourably to hiring a human financial advisor.

Popular robo-advisors include Nutmeg, Moneyfarm, Betterment, Wealthfront, Wealthsimple, etc.

iii. **Choose your stock investment yourself:** If your investments needs are simple i.e. adhere to the simple rules of asset allocation, use index funds, automate finances where possible, and you won't cross over £1

The Beauty of Compounding

million in assets any time soon, I believe you can certainly manage your finances and investments yourself.

However, complexity is added when you begin to consider your personal values and priorities. Many investors opt-out of the DIY route when they factor in the timing involved. A friend once told me he would rather choose to spend his precious time on higher priorities, such as family, health, or personal goal, than spending it on investment research and financial planning.

The advantage of choosing your stock investment yourself is that you will save on investment advisor fees. You will be in full control with complete freedom to make your own decisions. You will also learn about managing money and about finance in general (if you like that sort of thing).

On the flip side, your portfolio may not be balanced properly to accommodate market fluctuations. Or worse, you could make very expensive mistakes, such as paying high hidden fees, miss tax savings or make poor investment choices.

Determining which of these three options is best for you depends on your goals, needs, knowledge and current financial situation. To decide which is right for you, think of how complicated your finances are, think of how much money you have to invest, think of how much time you can

Page 98 of 168

allocate to investment research, and finally think of your level of sophistication and interest.

If you would like a little help, opening an account through a robo-advisor is a sensible option.

Step 2: Choose an investing account:

To invest in the stock market, you need an investment account. This is also known as a brokerage account.

A brokerage account is easily opened online; typically, a quick and painless process that only takes minutes. These accounts will offer you the quickest and least expensive path to buying and selling securities like stocks, bonds, and mutual funds. They are offered by companies such as Vanguard, Fidelity, Hargreaves Lansdown, Charles Schwab, Robinhood, and many others.

Just like a normal bank account, you can transfer money into and out of a brokerage account easily. And in addition to this capability, you will also have access to the stock market and other investments.

You don't need a lot of money to open a brokerage account. In fact, many brokerage firms allow you to open an account with no initial deposit. However, you will need to fund the account before you purchase investments. You can do that by transferring money from your current or savings account, or from another investment account.

You own the money and investments in your investment account, and you can sell investments at any time. The brokerage only holds your account and acts as an intermediary between you and the investments you want to purchase. There is no limit on the number of brokerage accounts you can have or the amount of money you can deposit into a taxable brokerage account each year.

In the UK, apart from the standard brokerage account, you can also open an investment individual savings account, also known as Stock and Shares ISA. This is a tax-efficient investment account that allows you to invest in a wide range of shares, funds, investment trusts and bonds. This means you don't have to pay income tax or capital gains tax on the money you earn from your investments made through the ISA, up to a certain limit (currently £20,000 this 2021/22 tax year).

Roth IRA is the USA's closest equivalent of the UK Stock and Shares ISA. It's an individual retirement account that provides tax-free growth and withdrawals. And like the UK stock and shares ISA, it has a contribution limit and threshold.

You don't need a lot of money to open a brokerage account. In fact, many brokerage firms allow you to open an account with no initial deposit.

Step 3: Stock investing or fund investing?

Before answering this question, let's quickly define these three investing terms: Mutual Fund, Index fund, and Exchange-Traded Funds.

i.   **Mutual Fund:** This is a type of financial vehicle made up of a pool of money collected from many investors to invest in securities like stocks, bonds, money market instruments, and other assets. Mutual funds are operated by professional money managers, who allocate the fund's assets and attempt to produce capital gains or income for the fund's investors after taking a fee.

Investing in a mutual fund is a good way to avoid some of the complicated decision-making involved in investing in individual stocks. Mutual funds offer diversified holdings which makes them very attractive. The cost of trading is spread over all mutual fund investors, thereby lowering the cost per individual.

ii. **Index Funds:** are one of the types of stock investments that diversify your investment across multiple stocks. In effect, investors who buy shares of an index fund own shares of stock in dozens, hundreds, or even thousands of different companies indirectly.

Unlike mutual funds, index funds are passively managed i.e. not overseen by a money manager. Because of this, less fees are involved, and costs are low.

iii.   **Exchange-Traded Funds (ETF):** ETFs are baskets of assets traded like securities. They can be bought and sold on an open exchange, as opposed to mutual funds, which are only priced at the end of the day.

You have more control over what price you purchase them at, and they typically carry lower fees than the equivalent mutual fund. ETFs can track not just an index, but an industry, a commodity or even another fund.

Now that we've defined all these investing terminologies, let's tackle the question: **"Stock investing or Fund investing?"**

I will say you can invest in individual stocks if you have the time and desire to thoroughly research the financial market, evaluate stocks on an ongoing basis, and if you stay on top of how the overall economy is doing.

On the other hand, if things like quarterly earnings reports and mathematical calculations sound unappealing to you, there's absolutely nothing wrong with taking a more passive approach and invest in funds - index funds or ETFs. These funds provide exposure to a broad basket of stocks and diversification in one purchase. S&P 500 is an example; when you buy an S&P 500 index fund or ETF, you're buying 500 stocks in a single fund, so that's a pretty easy way to get exposure to a lot of different companies.

In conclusion, whether you go the individual stock route or the fund route, make sure you pick a strategy that will not keep you up at night or cause you to panic sell during an economic downturn.

Funds provide exposure to a broad basket of stocks and diversification in one purchase.

Step 4: Determine how much to invest:

The stock market is no place for money that you might need within the next five years, at a minimum. Investing for the future is important, but so is making sure you can afford today. Your emergency fund or money you would need immediate access to must not be invested in the stock market. Time allows your money to grow and bounce back from short-term market fluctuations.

One of the many misconceptions about investing is that you need a lot of money to start. This is totally untrue; once you have a little money to play with, you can invest. Stocks move in percentages, not in amount; even if you only have a few pounds or dollars to spare, your money will grow with compound interest. The sooner you start investing with what little you have, the greater your chances of eventually having a lot of money to work with.

The ability to invest in companies with fractional or partial shares has also made investing with a small amount feasible. Instead of investing in a full share, you can buy a fraction of a share. Investing in a high-priced stock like Amazon, for instance, can be done for a few dollars instead of shelling out the price for one full share, which, as I write this book (April 2021) is 3,340.88 USD.

I always recommend you start your investment journey small and then work your way up over time. Set realistic investing priorities that are within your budget. Choose index funds over individual stocks to fully diversify your portfolio. Look into fractional shares. Investors with million-pound portfolios don't always start out rich, they got there by consistently investing the little money they have wisely. And over time, they successfully made their money work for them. You too can do the same. Start with what you have, your future self will thank you!

Step 5: Optimise your investment portfolio:

Watching your money grow as the stock market surges upward brings an amazing feeling. But if things turn difficult and the stock market dips, always remember that you are not alone. Every investor (including Warren Buffett) goes through the same up and down rough patches of the stock market.

The key to coming out ahead in the long-term is to always remember that you are investing for the long haul. Once you're familiar with the stock purchasing process, take the time to dig into other areas of the investment world and optimise your investment portfolio. Opening a brokerage account and buying stocks is a great first step, but it is really just the beginning of your investment journey.

The key to coming out ahead in the long-term is to always remember that you are investing for the long haul.

12. Real Estate Investing

Real estate has been one of the most dependable ways to become wealthy. And many of today's millionaires say it's still a smart investment, for a variety of reasons.

For one thing, investing in real estate gives you a way to diversify your investment portfolio. Real estate investors make money through rental income, appreciation, and profits generated by business activities that depend on the property. The benefits of investing in real estate include passive income, stable cash flow, tax advantages, diversification, and leverage.

There are a variety of ways to invest in real estate: buy REITs (Real Estate Investment Trust), buy homes, flip houses, business buildings, apartments, farms and trailer parks, to name a few. The options are many, let's deep dive into some of them.

i. Buy REITs (Real Estate Investment Trust):

A Real Estate Investment Trust, or REIT, is like a mutual fund in that it takes the funds of many investors and invests them in a collection of income-generating real estate properties. REIT allow you to invest in real estate without the physical real estate.

When you invest in REIT, you are investing in companies that hold physical property and as such own a piece of those properties. REITs tend to pay high dividends, which makes them a common investment in retirement. Investors who don't need or want the regular income can automatically reinvest those dividends to grow their investment further.

There are three types of REITs: Equity, Mortgage and Hybrid REITs.

- **Equity REITs:** Equity REITs own and manage income-producing real estate. Revenues are generated primarily through rents (not by reselling properties).

- **Mortgage REITs:** Mortgage REITs lend money to real estate owners and operators either directly through mortgages and loans, or indirectly through the acquisition of mortgage-backed securities. Their earnings are generated primarily by the net interest margin. This model makes them potentially sensitive to interest rate increases.

- **Hybrid REITs:** These REITs use the investment strategies of both equity and mortgage REITs, i.e. owns properties and holds mortgages

Without having to buy, manage, or finance any properties yourself, investing in a REIT reduces the barriers of entry common to property real estate investment. It is advisable that new investors stick to publicly-traded REITs, which you can purchase through brokerage firms. For that, you'll need a brokerage account.

Below are some common examples of REITs mutual fund

- Vanguard Real Estate Index Fund (VNQ)
- iShares U.S. Real Estate ETF (IYR)
- Fidelity MSCI Real Estate Index ETF
- iShares Global REIT
- Schwab U.S. REIT ETF (SCHH)

You don't need a lot of money and you don't need to worry about maintaining properties with REITs. While you won't make as much money from property appreciation, you can receive a steady income through this form of investing.

ii. Rental Property:

This is the traditional method of buying a property and renting it out to tenants. This is also known as Buy-To-Let property investment, which is very different from owning your own home. When you buy-to-let, you become a landlord or landlady. You are then effectively running a small business – one with important legal responsibilities.

To buy a rental property, you can use your own cash or take out a buy-to-let mortgage with a cash deposit. Every investment comes with risks and returns and buy-to-let is not exempted from such. If you can't find tenants (or if you can't charge the rent you expected), you might not be able to cover your mortgage repayments.

If house prices fall, the value of your property is likely to fall as well. You might not be able to sell it for as much as you hoped. If you have to sell and the sale price doesn't cover the whole mortgage, you'll have to make up the difference. Major repairs or difficult tenants might also increase your costs unexpectedly.

The kinds of consumer protections that cover most investments don't apply to buy-to-let properties. So, it's very important that you find out everything you can before you commit to a property and a mortgage.

Once you buy a rental property, you can earn a profit in two ways: rental yield and capital growth. Rental yield is what your tenant(s) pay in rent, minus any maintenance and running costs, like repairs and agent fees. Capital growth is the profit you earn if you sell your property for more than you paid for it.

Real estate investors make money through rental income, appreciation, and profits generated by business activities that depend on the property.

iii. <u>House Hacking:</u>

House hacking allows you to live in your investment property while renting out rooms or units.

Judith didn't intend to become a real estate investor when she bought her first rental property at age 22. She just finished her bachelor's degree at the University of Manchester and was planning to do her postgraduate degree at the same university. Judith's parents opened a trust fund for her when she was little, which they have been generously contributing to for years. With this windfall cash at Judith's disposal, she figured that buying a property would be better than renting.

Judith found a four-bedroom, four-bathroom semi-detached house that was set up student-housing style near the university. She bought the property, lived in one bedroom, and rented out the other three. The setup covered all her expenses and brought in an extra £200 per month in cash – this is a cool cash inflow for any graduate student's standard.

Judith is now 30 years old and steadily on her path to financial independence. She attributes her financial success to catching the real estate bug when she was 22. That experience of buying her first property launched her into the world of real estate. She currently has four rentals and she's always on the lookout for houses to hack.

The strategy Judith used in entering the real estate market is called **house hacking** - a term coined by BiggerPockets, an online resource for real estate investors. It means you are occupying your investment property, either by renting out rooms, as Judith did or by renting out units in a multi-unit building.

iv.   <u>Flipping Properties:</u>

This is a strategy where you invest in an under-priced home in need of a little love, renovate it as inexpensively as possible and then resell it for a profit.

Let's look at Mr and Mrs Coker's flipping journey:
In Year 1, they invested £100,000 in a piece of real estate. They fixed it up, and after all expenses were factored in, they sold the property and made a profit of £15,000 on the flip. This couple made a return of 15% on their investment.

In Year 2, they invest £115,000 in another piece of real estate. They fixed it up and earned another 15% return, but this time their profit was £17,250! This couple can go on and on in this cycle and this is how their wealth compounds with time.

Let me quickly call out that there's a bigger element of risk in the flipping strategy. So much of the math behind flipping requires a very accurate estimate of how much repairs are going to cost, which is not an easy thing to do. The other risk of flipping is that the longer you hold the property, the less money you make because you're paying a mortgage without bringing in any income.

> # "Landlords grow rich in their sleep without working, risking or economizing."
> ## - John Stuart Mill

v. Real Estate Crowdfunding

Real estate crowdfunding is a new way to invest in commercial real estate, and it has exploded in popularity in recent years. It involves a group of investors who each contribute money to a specific real estate deal.

The general idea behind real estate crowdfunding is that when a developer or experienced real estate professional identifies an investment opportunity, they don't always have the ability (or desire) to completely fund the investment on their own. So, they'll allow individual investors to contribute some of the project's capital in order to raise enough money to execute their plan.

There are three key players in any crowdfunded real estate investment opportunity: the sponsor, the crowdfunding platform and the investor.

The sponsor is the individual or company that identifies, plans, and oversees the investment itself. The deal's sponsor will facilitate the purchase of the asset, arrange for any contractors or other needed work, arrange financing, and take responsibility for the eventual sale of the property. Sponsors do contribute towards the project's funding and are also entitled to a certain share of any profits they earn for the deal's investors.

The crowdfunding platform is where the sponsor finds investors to raise the necessary capital for a project. I consider the platform as the go-between between investors and sponsors. The platform will ensure a deal meets certain standards, advertise deals to potential investors, guarantee that investors meet the requirements for investment, and deal with regulatory issues. The platform will also collect investors' funds on behalf of the deal sponsor.

The third key player in crowdfunding is **the investor**. Investors contribute some of the required capital in exchange for a share of the profits from the deal. An investor may get some sort of income distributions and/or be entitled to a proportional pay out from an eventual profitable sale.

Like any investment opportunity, real estate crowdfunding isn't a perfect fit for everyone. There are several potential pros and cons of real estate crowdfunding that should be considered before deciding whether it's right for you.

vi.　Rent out a room:

If you have just a single property, you could consider renting out a room rather than renting out the property as a whole. Sites like Airbnb are often used for this. You don't have to take on a long-term tenant, potential renters are pre-screened by Airbnb, and the company's host guarantee protects against damages.

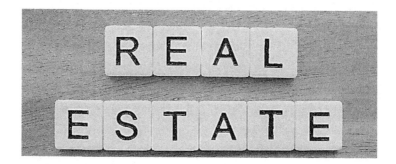

"Success in real estate starts when you believe you are worthy of it."
- Michael Ferrara

In conclusion, I will say that the best real estate investments are the ones that best serve you, the investor. Think about how much time you have, how much capital you're willing to invest and whether you want to be the one who deals with household issues when they inevitably come up. If you don't have DIY skills and don't have much time, consider investing in real estate through a REIT or a crowdfunding platform rather than directly in a property.

Real estate is a distinct asset class that's simple to understand and can enhance the risk-and-return profile of an investor's portfolio. On its own, real estate offers steady passive income, cash flow, tax breaks, equity building, competitive risk-adjusted returns, and a hedge against inflation. Real estate can also enhance a portfolio by lowering volatility through diversification, whether you invest in physical properties or REITs.

Despite all the benefits of investing in real estate, there are drawbacks. One of the main ones is the lack of liquidity (or the relative difficulty in converting an asset into cash and cash into an asset). Unlike a stock or bond transaction, which can be completed in seconds, a real estate transaction can take months to close. Even with the help of a broker, it can take a few weeks of work just to find the right counterparty.

13. Cryptocurrency Investing

One of the standard rules of investing is to never invest in something you don't understand. For a very long time after embarking on my investing journey, I was very wary of cryptocurrency investing. I simply didn't understand how it works. Let's begin this chapter by defining what exactly is Cryptocurrency.

Cryptocurrency is an intangible digital asset that uses a highly sophisticated type of encryption called cryptography to secure and verify transactions as well as to control the creation of new units of currency. It is designed to work as a decentralised medium of exchange, independent of a financial institution or any other central authority.

Cryptocurrencies have gained a lot of interest in recent years as an investment vehicle. However, they remain an incredibly risky investment due to many unknown factors; there is the possibility of government regulation, its susceptibility to fraud, and the possibility that the cryptocurrency will never see widespread acceptance as a form of payment.

The world of crypto investing is still relatively uncharted territory. Even though currencies like bitcoin have grown in popularity, it is still a highly volatile and highly risky investment.

For example, at the start of 2017, Bitcoin was trading under $1,000. By the end of that year, it had jumped to nearly $20,000. By late 2018, however, it was back down to nearly $3,000, wiping out billions of dollars from the total cryptocurrency market value. While that can mean big returns, it can also mean big losses. As I write this book (April 2021), Bitcoin is trading at $56,771. See prior years trend image below:

The rise and fall of bitcoin
Exchange rate, $

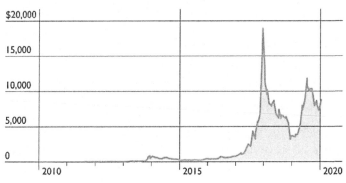

Source: Hargreaves Lansdown

While Bitcoin is the most well-known cryptocurrency, it is not the only one. Other major types of cryptocurrencies include: Ethereum, Ripple, Bitcoin Cash, LiteCoin, Dash, Zcash and Monero. Cryptocurrencies can be used to pay for goods and services, as well as for investing in some part of the world. In this respect, we can say that they are similar to physical currencies. But unlike traditional physical currencies, cryptocurrencies are not issued by a central authority, neither are they considered legal tender. The vast majority of cryptocurrencies are not backed by a government or legal entity.

My Cryptocurrency Investing Experience

Financial experts advise that people looking to invest in cryptocurrencies like bitcoin should allocate a small amount of their portfolio that they'd be okay with losing entirely. And this is the advice I am implementing personally.

In my quest for knowledge, I have been researching and learning about digital currencies with a specific focus on cryptocurrencies – Bitcoin, Ethereum, Bitcoin Cash, etc. I was mentally ready and financially prepared that a crash could happen again – even tomorrow. And with some **free money** I had on the side, I did put some into trading in this risky digital asset. See chapter 14 for an introduction to trading.

My personal decision to trade in Bitcoin was more of the thrill of investing in it and also to observe what else is happening out there in the world of investing. I like to see the money I'm using to purchase bitcoin (which is so insignificant in comparison with my overall investment portfolio), as money that could go away tomorrow, and the small amount will not keep me up at night.

My strategy so far is simple, I buy the underlying asset on a trading platform when the prices are low, and I sell when the prices are high. Buying the underlying asset involves exchanging your money for cryptoasset bitcoin tokens. The trading company then purchases the tokens on your behalf and registers them in a segregated account under your name.

If the price of the cryptoasset rises while you own it, you'll profit. However, if the price falls, you'll generate a loss. As of today (15th April 2021), 1 bitcoin costs $56,771 (equivalent to £40,965). Despite this high purchase price, one can buy as little as $50 of bitcoin because there is the ability to buy fractional shares.

I won't still recommend bitcoin to beginner investors. But if you do decide to put some money in bitcoin, I will say start small, do your research, and learn about it. Be prepared to lose some or all of your money. Crypto is not conventional investing. They are also not regulated by the UK watchdog, adding another layer of risk.

While Bitcoin's acolytes tend to focus on the future of blockchain technology, it's worth paying close attention to this currency's past. Also, unlike most other investments, Bitcoin doesn't pay out cash to its owners like a stock pays dividends or a bond interest. That means its value only increases when more people want to own it.

Coinbase and Binance are two of the world's largest bitcoin trading platforms. They are touted as the easy and fast way for new users to purchase various cryptocurrencies such as bitcoin. Other ways to buy include the digital currency app Ziglu and on the investment platform eToro. Be wary of the fees involved in cryptocurrency trading. Transaction fees, deposit fees, withdrawal fees, trading fees and escrow fees are a few percent of the total transaction value.

"Well, I think it is working. There may be other currencies like it that may be even better. But in the meantime, there's a big industry around Bitcoin. People have made fortunes off Bitcoin, some have lost money. It is volatile, but people make money off of volatility too."
– Richard Branson

The Beauty of Compounding

14. Introduction to Trading

After several years of embarking on my long-term investment journey, I started looking into trading. When people tell you that investing is gambling, what they really mean is that trading is gambling. I've heard and seen so many people lose lots of money in trading. But is trading that bad? I often ask myself.

I knew trading, unlike investing, is a short-term dealing. I also knew that I will not be able to educate others and write this chapter if I don't venture into trading myself. So, I summoned courage, took the leap of faith, and started trading. But before embarking on this new journey, I wrote myself two personal mantras:

Oyenike:

- **Never invest in what will keep you up at night.**
- **Never invest more than you can afford to lose.**

So, everything you're reading in this section is documentation of my personal journey and experience with trading. I am still on the learning path, and as with my other personal finance experiences, I'm in a school where no one ever graduates from!

Let me start by saying trading is not the same as investing. Even though both investors and traders seek profits through market participation, investors seek larger returns over an extended period (long-term) through buying and holding. Traders, on the other hand, take advantage of both rising and falling markets to enter and exit positions over a shorter timeframe, making smaller, more frequent profits.

<u>Definition of Trading</u>

In the simplest term, trading is when you are constantly buying and selling securities, trying to avoid losses, having a goal of earning a higher return. Trading is about making frequent, short-term transactions with the goal of "beating the market", or generating greater returns than you'd expect to receive by buying and holding over a longer time frame.

Short-term transaction can range from immediate buying and selling a security within minutes, up to transactions that last weeks or months. While long-term investors often aim for an average rate of annual return of 7-8%, a trading goal may be a 7-8% gain every day or every month.

Just a quick pause to define the word **'Security'**. The securities I am referencing in this chapter are the different asset classes - like stocks, commodities, forex, and other types of easily liquidated assets.

Traders fall into one of four categories differentiated by their trading style, the time period in which they typically hold their securities, the amount of time they can dedicate to trading, their level of trading experience, and their risk tolerance. The four types of traders are:

i. **Scalp Traders:**
   Hold securities for just a few seconds or minutes.

ii. **Day Traders:**
   Hold securities throughout the day, but not overnight.

iii. **Swing Traders:**
   Hold securities for days or weeks.

iv. **Position Traders:**
   Hold securities for months or years.

I see myself as a Swing Trader. My trading account positions typically last two to six days but could also last as long as two weeks. The goal of swing trading is to identify an overall trend and capture larger gains within it.

Trading Strategy

There are three common trading strategies: Buy low sell high, Buy high sell higher, and Short selling.

i. Buy Low, Sell High:

The term "buy low, sell high" comes into play often when trading, as traders aim to turn a profit in a short period of time, by closely monitoring price changes.

Traders search for the point where they believe the market has hit its lowest point, buy a share, then sell once it goes up. They often use technical analysis to help take advantage of a security's current trend. By identifying both the trend's direction and its strength, traders can hopefully improve their trades.

ii. Buy High, Sell Higher:

In this strategy, when traders see the market is going up in an upward trajectory, for the short-term, they buy into the market and sell it higher. They have no reason to believe the market will go lower in the near future.

The stocks that are the biggest winners must trade at their highs quite often. A stock like Apple (AAPL) or Amazon (AMZN) cannot go from $6 to $1,000 unless it's trading at its highs constantly. If a trader uses a "buy low, sell high" approach, they will never be in the best stocks when they are seeing their biggest growth.

iii. <u>Short Selling:</u>

In this strategy, a trader borrows a stock, sells the stock, and then buys the stock back to return it to the lender. Short sellers are betting that the stock they sell will drop in price. If the stock does drop after selling, the short seller buys it back at a lower price and returns it to the lender. The difference between the sell price and the buy price is the profit.

Short selling involves amplified risk. The strategy speculates on the decline in a stock or other security's price. When an investor short sells, they can theoretically lose an infinite amount of money because a stock's price can keep rising forever. This is therefore an advanced strategy that should only be undertaken by experienced traders and investors.

I have tried the Buy Low, Sell High and the Buy High, Sell Higher strategies. Short selling is simply not for me – I'm a newbie in trading!

"Buy when everyone else is selling and hold when everyone else is buying. This is not merely a catchy slogan. It is the very essence of successful investments"
- J. Paul Getty

Trading Platforms

Trading platforms form the crucial bridge between traders and their chosen financial market. Online trading platforms are frequently offered by brokers either for free or at a discount rate in exchange for maintaining a funded account and/or making a specified number of trades per month. The best trading platforms offer a mix of robust features and low fees.

Trading platforms often come bundled with other features, such as real-time quotes, charting tools, news feeds, and even premium research. Platforms may also be specifically tailored to specific markets, such as stocks, currencies, options, or futures markets. Traders use a variety of different trading platforms depending on their trading style and volume.

There are so many trading platforms out there. I have only used one so far on my trading journey, **"eToro"**, and that's the one I will share my experience on in this book. Other popular trading platforms out there are: Interactive Brokers, TDAmeritrade, Robinhood, Plus500, Libertex, CedarFX, Trading 212, etc.

eToro Trading Platform

I've never tried any other trading platforms apart from eToro, so I have nothing else to compare it with. But my experience so far is summarised below:

- The platform is perfect if you are just starting out in the world of online trading. This is because the platform is simple to use, and it supports small stakes.

- Unlike some other trading platforms that require a very high deposit before you can trade, eToro's minimum deposit is just $200 and you trade from $25 upwards.

- Every financial market at eToro can be traded on a commission-free basis. You don't need to pay any ongoing fees either, so eToro is a great trading platform for those seeking a low-cost provider.

- In terms of what assets you can trade, eToro supports several asset classes. This covers 2,400 stocks across 17 different markets. For example, you can buy shares in companies based in the US, Canada, UK, Europe, Hong Kong, etc.

- eToro allows you to access over 250 ETFs and 16 cryptocurrencies. eToro supports all commodities types like gold, silver, and even oil and natural gas. eToro also offers a huge forex trading facility.

- eToro has an excellent CopyPortfolio feature where you can benefit from a professionally managed investment strategy. This means that the team at eToro can buy and sell assets on your behalf.

eToro is a safe and regulated, zero-commission stockbroker. It has a simple, easy-to-use trading platform, and a great mobile trading app.

Is trading right for you?

Trading offers the opportunity to actively participate in the market, far more frequently than you would be investing. If you enjoy the process of researching stocks and are comfortable taking calculated risks as you closely navigate the market, you might incorporate elements of trading into your overall investment strategy.

Before you venture into trading, you need to understand that any short-term trading strategy comes with considerable risk of loss, and positive returns are never guaranteed. Also, trading can be very time-consuming as active trading requires a lot of time spent researching companies and stocks, as well as staying up-to-date with and managing one's portfolio.

Part 4 Recap

- Retirement investing refers to the financial strategies of saving, investment, and ultimately the distribution of money meant to sustain one's self after paid work ends, i.e. during retirement.

- Stock market investing is a long-term process that could help you manage your finances. The stock market is a place where buyers and sellers meet to sell shares – each one a tiny part of a company listed on an exchange. In return for your cash, a business offers you a share in its future, i.e. you own tiny slice of that company and become a 'shareholder'.

- Real estate investing involves the purchase, ownership, management, rental and/or sale of real estate for profit. There are a variety of ways to invest in real estate: buy REITs (Real Estate Investment Trust), rental property, house hacking, flipping properties, crowdfunding, etc.

- Cryptocurrencies are also known as crypto coins, digital currency and cryptoassets. Examples include Bitcoin, Ethereum and Litecoin. Cryptocurrencies have gained a lot of interest in recent years as an investment vehicle. However, they remain an incredibly risky investment due to many unknown factors like volatility, non-acceptance as payment, unregulated and unprotected by organisations like the FCA or FSCS.

- Stock trading involves constant buying and selling of securities, trying to avoid losses, and having a goal of earning a higher return. Trading is all about making frequent, short-term transactions with the goal of "beating the market", or generating greater returns than you'd expect to receive by buying and holding over a longer time frame.

PART 5:

INVESTMENT STRATEGIES

15. Dollar-Cost Averaging

Dollar-Cost averaging (DCA) is an investment strategy in which an investor consistently builds wealth over a long period. Investors use DCA to reduce the impact of short-term volatility by spreading out investment purchases and buying at regular intervals and in roughly equal amounts regardless of the asset's price.

By making regular investments with the same amount of money each time, you will buy more of an investment when its price is low and less of the investment when its price is high. DCA therefore "smooths" out the purchase price over time and removes much of the detailed work of attempting to time the market in order to make purchases of equities at the best prices.

A perfect example of dollar-cost averaging is its use in the workplace retirement plan (we discussed retirement investing in Chapter 10). This plan allows employees to consistently contribute a portion of their pre-tax paycheck to tax-deferred investments. The amount the employee has contributed is then invested in their investment choices regardless of the fund's price.

Dollar-cost averaging can also be used outside of retirement investing e.g. in mutual or index fund accounts. An example of this would be investing £200 per month in an index fund that tracks the performance of a broad market index, such as the S&P 500. In some months, the index will be priced high, meaning fewer shares would be purchased for the £200 investment. In other months, when the index is low, £200 would purchase a greater number of shares.

In the long run, the simplicity of the DCA strategy, combined with the fact that it protects investors from the temptation of buying high and selling low, will ultimately lead to better results than trying to time the market on each purchase.

Dollar-Cost Averaging is one of the best strategies for beginner investors looking to trade in Exchange Traded Funds (ETFs). I can't recommend it enough. Implementing it will reduce your anxiety about investing. And those emotional benefits make it a great choice for you!

Investment strategy refers to a set of principles designed to help an individual investor achieve their financial and investment goals.

16. The Rule of 72

The Rule of 72 is a quick way to figure how long it will take for your savings or investments to double in value, assuming a fixed annual rate of return and no additional contribution.

Learning how to invest is stressful to many people, so stressful that many people don't make it to the next step of figuring out how to project the growth of their investments - even though that's crucial to their financial success.

So, what if you could plug some numbers into a simple formula and find out how long it would take for your investments to double? That's exactly what the Rule of 72 does.

The formula is simple: 72 divided by interest rate equals the number of years it will take for your investments to double.

The Rule of 72 Formula

$$t \approx \frac{72}{r}$$

t = Number of periods it will take for the investment to double

r = The interest rate per period expressed as a percentage

You will notice the formula uses the "approximately equals" symbol ($\approx$) rather than the regular "equals" symbol ($=$). That's because this formula offers an estimate rather than an exact amount, and it's most accurate when used on investments that earn a typical rate of 6% to 10%.

For example, if your money is earning a 12% interest rate, it will take 6 years for your money to double (72 divided by 12 equals 6).

Or, if your money is earning a 3% interest rate, it will take 24 years for your money to double (72 divided by 3 equals 24).

And if your money is earning a measly 1% interest rate, it will take a whopping 72 years to double it (72 divided by 1 equals 72).

It's important to note that the "Rule of 72" is a useful guide and not iron-clad law. The rule assumes that your money compounds annually, meaning that once a year your interest gets added to your principal and the entire amount is reinvested.

The Rule of 72 offers a quick and easy way for investors to project the growth of their investments. By showing how quickly you can double your money with minimal effort, this rule beautifully demonstrates the magic of compounding for building wealth.

17. The Rule of 115

The Rule of 115 is used to figure out how long it will take for an investment to triple in value. It follows the same process as the Rule of 72. Here, 115 is divided by the interest rate. The quotient is the amount of time it will take you to triple your money.

The Rule of 115 Formula

$$t \approx \frac{115}{r}$$

t = Number of periods it will take for the investment to triple

r = The interest rate per period expressed as a percentage

For example, if your money earns a 10% interest rate, it will take 11.5 years for your money to triple (115 divided by 10 equals 11.5).

Or, if your money is earning a 5% interest rate, it will take 23 years for your money to triple (115 divided by 5 equals 23)

And if your money is earning a measly 1% interest rate, it will take 115 years for your money to triple (115 divided by 1 equals 115)

The "Rule of 115" is a useful guide and not iron-clad laws. If you understand and apply this rule to your personal finance, you're less likely to settle for opportunities that don't give you an advantage. You're also less likely to take on debt that might take forever to pay off.

This rule work because it's a simple manipulation of the compound interest formula. The more interest your money earns, the more your money will work for you. However, this assumes you reinvest the interest.

Getting a sense of how compound interest can potentially grow your portfolio is enough to light a fire under you and get you started investing as early as possible.

The power of compound interest is just amazing. "He who understands it earns it ... he who doesn't ... pays it." — Albert Einstein.

18. Diversification

Diversification is a technique that reduces risk by allocating investments among various financial instruments, industries and other categories. Diversification comes from this simple mantra we are all familiar with: **"don't put all your eggs in the same basket"**. This means if one of your investments performs poorly, your other investments will hopefully perform better to deliver good returns.

We looked at asset classes in Chapter 9. Diversification aims at spreading investments across a variety of asset classes, like equity, fixed income, real estate and tangible assets, but also across a variety of risk concentration, like geographic and industry sectors. Different asset classes rarely react in the same way to adverse events. A combination of asset classes will therefore reduce your portfolio's sensitivity to market swings.

While individual asset classes can suffer severe declines, it's very rare that any two or three assets with very different sources of risk and return, like government bonds, gold and equities, would experience declines of this magnitude at the same time. So even if stocks tanked 20%, your bonds and gold would keep your portfolio from falling as far. This is why diversification is important in your investments.

It is important to note that not all investment risks are diversifiable. There are two categories of investment risks; one is undiversifiable, and the other is diversifiable.

Undiversifiable risks are also known as "systematic" or "market risk". These are risk of losses on financial investments caused by adverse price movements. This type of risk is not specific to a particular company or industry, and it cannot be eliminated or reduced through diversification. It is a risk that investors must accept. Examples of undiversifiable risks are changes in interest rate, inflation rates, exchange rates, foreign exchange fluctuations, political instability and war, etc.

Diversifiable risks, on the other hand, are unsystematic risks. They are specific to a company, industry, market, economy or country; and they can be reduced through diversification. The most common sources of unsystematic risk are business risk and financial risk. Thus, the aim is to invest in various assets so that they will not all be affected the same way by market events.

The benefit of diversification in your investments is to minimize the risk of a bad event taking out your entire portfolio. When you keep a high percentage of your portfolio in a single type of investment, you risk losing it if that investment sours. There's also the opportunity cost of not being diversified. If you're not diversified, you may miss out on growth opportunities in a different asset class that you're not exposed to.

How Do I Diversify My Portfolio?

There are several ways to diversify your portfolio, but the same rule always applies.

i. **Diversification by asset classes:** Having a mix of different asset types will help you spread risk. The theory behind this approach is that the values of different assets can move independently and often for different reasons. A new investor's diverse portfolio should include cash, stocks, bonds, exchange-traded funds and mutual funds.

ii. **Diversification by sector:** once you've decided on the assets classes you want in your portfolio, you can diversify further by investing in different sectors, preferably those that aren't highly correlated to each other. For example, if the healthcare sector suffers from a downturn, this will not necessarily have an impact on the precious metals sector. This helps to make sure your portfolio is protected from dips in certain industries.

iii. **Diversification by region:** Investing in different regions and countries can reduce the impact of stock market movements. This means that you're not just affected by the economic conditions of one country and one government's economic policies. Developed markets, such as the UK and US, aren't as volatile as those in emerging markets like China, India and Russia.

Investing abroad can help you diversify, but you need to be comfortable with the levels of risk involved.

Diversification is not a one-time task. You should check your portfolio often and make changes accordingly when the risk level is not consistent with your financial goals or strategy. The process of checking and realigning the weight of the different assets in your portfolio to maintain your desired asset allocation based on your risk appetite is called **Portfolio Rebalancing**. I recommend rebalancing your portfolio at least once a year.

Robo-advisor such as Betterment automatically rebalances portfolio for investors. If you don't want to spend the time to manually rebalance your portfolio, you could consider robo-advisor.

One way to balance risk and reward in your investment portfolio is to diversify your assets.

19. Investing Returns

Returns are the profit you earn from your investments. Depending on where you put your money, it could make money and be paid in three different ways: appreciation, dividend, and capital gains.

i. Asset appreciation:

Asset appreciation occurs when the value of an asset increases over time. Appreciation can be used to refer to an increase in any type of assets, such as a stock, bond, currency, or real estate.

Using real estate, for example, let's say that you purchase a home in Birmingham for £150,000. Over the next ten years, the value of the home steadily rises. You have the home appraised, and it is found to be worth £250,000. This means that your asset has increased (or appreciated) £100,000 in value, which is a pretty nice return on your investment.

ii. Dividends from shares:

This is a way of earning returns on your investments or making money when you invest in the stock market. Dividends are profits the company distributes and pay out to investors based on the amount they own.

Most companies pay dividends in the form of cash, although you may hear of occasions when a company uses stock instead. It's important to understand that these dividend payments are never guaranteed. Dividends are only paid out of profits or reserves of a company. So, a loss-making company with no reserves cannot pay a dividend.

iii. Capital gains:

Capital gains are profits from the sale of an asset, such as shares of stock, a business, a parcel of land, or a work of art. It is the difference between the price you pay for an asset and the price you sell for.

For example, say Nicky purchased 10 shares of Amazon stock on March 10, 2016, at £300 per share. Two years later, on March 10, 2018, she sells all the shares at a price of £900 each. Assuming there were no fees associated with the sale, Nicky realized a capital gain of £6,000 (£900 * 10 - £300 * 10 = £6,000).

From the above example, you can see that a capital gain is only possible when the selling price of the asset is greater than the original purchase price. Capital gains are often subject to taxation, of which rates and exemptions may differ between countries.

Part 5 Recap

- Dollar-cost averaging (DCA) refers to the practice of dividing an investment of an equity up into multiple smaller investments of equal amounts, spaced out over regular intervals. It's an investment strategy that aims to reduce the impact of volatility on large purchases of financial assets such as equities.

- The Rule of 72 is a simple equation to help you determine how long an investment will take to double given a fixed interest rate. It's a shortcut that investors used to estimate if an investment will double your money quickly enough to be worth pursuing. It is calculated by dividing 72 by the interest rate.

- The Rule of 115 follows the Rule of 72. If doubling your money isn't good enough, the Rule of 115 will show you how long it will take to triple your money. The calculation is as simple as dividing 115 by your interest rate. The quotient is the amount of time it will take you to triple your money.

- Diversification is a technique that reduces risk by allocating investments across various financial instruments, industries, and other categories. It aims to maximize returns by investing in different areas that would each react differently to the same event.

- Three common ways of earning returns on an investment are: asset appreciation, dividend, and capital gains. Appreciation is an increase in the value of an asset over time. Dividends are profits a company distributes and pays out to investors based on the amount they own. Capital gains are profits from the sale of an asset when the selling price of the asset is greater than the original purchase price.

PART 6:

INVESTING MISTAKES TO AVOID

The Beauty of Compounding

20. Pitfalls And Mistakes To Avoid

Many are hesitant to invest because of the fear of financial loss. I had this experience when I embarked on my investing journey; at the time, I found myself getting into a new world of unknowns.

Even experienced investors sometimes have investment fears; many have made tons of investment mistakes and lived through financial regrets. People make a bad decision, get carried away by emotions, and lose money because of situations outside of their control.

Fear is the biggest adversity when it comes to investing. Fear of losing money will stop people from even trying. This fear will also cause investors to panic and sell early, throwing away future returns. And if we add to this the fear of missing out (FOMO), which causes people to get greedy or act rashly, then we can see that fear is a dangerous two-headed beast that can hurt you both ways.

However, it is possible to beat investment fears and overcome adversity. I believe there are some actions we can take to reduce and if possible, eliminate investments fears and mistakes. I have listed a few pitfalls and mistakes to avoid if you want to be a successful investor and experience safe investing.

i. Not Investing at all:

The biggest mistake anyone can make is failing to invest at all. Cash is a depreciating asset because of inflation - inflation eats up the value of cash over time. However, investing in assets such as equities, bonds and commercial properties has proved the best way to grow capital and protect it from inflation over the long-term.

Anyone that is not investing is missing out tremendously. Early contributions are most valuable as they have the longest time to compound. The best time to invest was YESTERDAY. The next best time is TODAY. Do not delay. Start investing NOW!

ii. Lack of a plan:

Planning is an important step in the investing process. Diving straight into investing without a defined plan is one of the biggest mistakes made by investors.

Before embarking on your investing journey, make sure you have answers to these three questions:

- Why am I investing?
- How long am I investing for?
- What is my attitude to risk?

iii. Never invest in anything you don't understand:

Overestimating your abilities and knowledge is a recipe for disaster. You don't know everything. Invest in what you know. Study what you can learn and stick to it. If you don't understand something, don't blindly try it out. You must learn before you can earn. Every investment you make in yourself will pay you dividends for a lifetime.

Do what you know and remember the first rule of investing is not to lose money. The more you know about investing, the fewer mistakes you'll likely make, and the better will be your investment performance. So, invest in your financial education. It will pay you dividends for a lifetime.

iv. Failing to diversify:

By diversifying, you avoid investing aggressively into one class. If your investments weigh heavy in one area during a market rise or fall, the dynamics could devastate your portfolio. The first part of a diversification strategy consists of mixing asset classes by holding various stocks, bonds, cash, real estate, etc.

The second part of a properly diversified portfolio is mixing within asset classes. Opting in to a good mix of small-cap, large-cap, international, and industry sector-diverse equities is wise. While a market decline may affect a certain stock or sector, a gain in another might offset the loss. Diversification must never be ignored when investing.

v. Get comfortable being uncomfortable:

Determining how much you are willing to lose, and how much you can financially afford, are key questions you need to answer. Not only to ensure you sleep well but to also reduce panic decisions and support the long-term sustainability of your investment portfolio.

There will always be natural market fluctuations when investing. While watching your money go up and down like a rollercoaster can make you queasy and frantic, never make a decision to sell out because of fear. Get comfortable being uncomfortable when there's a slip in the investment performance.

vi. If something is too good to be true, it probably is:

Investing is not a get-rich-quick scheme. Investing doesn't make you rich overnight. It takes decades to grow wealth. If something is too good to be true, it probably is. It's tempting to look for the big wins, but on average victory goes to the steady and patient investors.

vii. Emotions are an investor's worst enemy:

While it sounds easy to just focus on the long-term, it is hard to do in reality because money is emotional. Emotional response to sell during downturns (crippled by fear of losing all), often makes an average investor to only buy after financial markets show a strong recent history of gains rather than investing consistently for the long-term.

Watch out for the three primary emotions that negatively impact investment returns: fear, greed, and impatience. Form an investing strategy based on your own unique financial goals and needs. Then automate it to continue operating regardless of the herd mentality and investor sentiment of the moment.

viii. Watch out for fees and associated costs:

The more you pay in fees and associated investing costs, the less of your returns you get to keep. When investing, always aim to keep your fees, charges, and costs low. If you're using a high commission fund manager and also investing in something that has high transaction charges, you are very likely to lose money.

ix. Ignore the noise:

With investing, noise is everywhere. There's always a line of people waiting to give you their opinion regardless of whether or not you wanted to hear it. The media too is never quiet; it loves to hype things while hitting the panic button hard.

If you pore over the latest market news, following every crash and recovery, you will give yourself a headache, and probably make a lot of bad investment decisions at the same time. Despite natural disasters, conflicts, referendums, and controversial presidents, markets always bounce back. There is a difference between staying informed about your investments and being obsessed with noise.

x. Attempting to time the market:

Market timing is the act of moving investment money in or out of a financial market or switching funds between asset classes based on predictive methods. The principle behind this is simple; buy when the market is low and sell when the market is high. This is unfortunately easier said than done. While timing the market seems like a good idea on paper, it rarely works out in practice.

So what should you do instead of market timing? First of all, stay calm and carry on. Stock market downturns are normal, they've happened many times in the past and bound to occur many more times in the future. Your best bet is to "buy and hold" while the market goes through its cycles. Whatever you do, don't sell your investments and convert them to cash with the plan to rebuy later when the market stabilises. This strategy is called "panic selling".

xi. Stock picking:

Randomly buying individual stocks or companies making the news through a recent high-profile IPO is rarely a good idea. By all means, you can allocate a small percentage of your budget to stock picking ideas if this is what you want. Stock picking should not form the foundation of your long-term investment strategy.

Beginner investors are better off looking at index funds and mutual funds, which comprise many hundreds of different companies from all over the world within a single fund. You won't have to worry about stocks bouncing back when the market dips. You won't have to worry about finding the 'right' companies, because you own them all, to begin with. Index and mutual funds allow you to enjoy market-matching returns for zero effort and near-zero cost.

xii. Withdrawing from your investment portfolio:

Investing is a long-term goal. And the only time I think is wise to withdraw from your investments portfolio is when you reach your goal. When you take money out of your investments early, you don't just lose the initial value of your withdrawal, you also lose the growth that money would have generated had it remained invested.

A friend recently told me that he's allowed to take money from his retirement investment whenever he needs it. And my response to him was this: 'Yes you're allowed, but just because you can doesn't mean you should'. If you dip into your pension pot or your 401(k) early, you will end up losing most of your money in early withdrawal fees and taxes.

xiii. <u>**Be kind to yourself and give yourself grace:**</u>

No investor is perfect. You will make mistakes along the way. Everyone does it. A friend told me she bought her first share of Alphabet at £150 and sold it a few months later for £300. If she had kept it, she would be sitting on a seven-figure investment today.

But that's the price paid for being ignorant and lack of education about the markets. Lesson learnt, then move on. Be kind to yourself when you make mistakes and don't compound them by quitting investing after a scare. And when the next bear market hits, be sure to use all the lessons learnt to keep your cool, save your sanity and grow your money with a long-term focus.

In conclusion, investors who recognize and avoid these common pitfalls give themselves an advantage in pursuing their investment goals. It's a lot easier to enjoy the investment process when you learn how to avoid committing some of the most common and expensive investment mistakes. Making money is more enjoyable than losing it. Steering clear of just one of these investment mistakes can literally make the difference between wealth and poverty.

With discipline and focus, you can strategically turn your investing dreams into financial realities.

Part 6 Recap

- Fear is the biggest adversity when it comes to investing. Fear of losing will stop people from even trying.

- Being a smart investor doesn't mean just being confident. It is not blind confidence that makes people winners. Being smart means having the knowledge and being prepared to react with confidence while investing.

- Not Investing at all, lack of a plan, failing to diversify, stock picking, attempting to time the market, not caring about fees, emotional response to market movement, hitting the panic button every time there is noise in the market, not giving yourself grace, etc are examples of common mistakes and pitfalls to avoid as a beginner investor.

- Investors who recognize and avoid these common pitfalls give themselves an advantage in pursuing their investment goals. It's a lot easier to enjoy the investment process when you learn how to avoid committing some of the most common and expensive investment mistakes.

The Beauty of Compounding

IN CLOSING

Congratulations! You've made it to the end of this book, and my hope is that you've learnt one or two things about investing. Knowing how money works and how to secure your finance are two of the most important things you'll ever need in life. You don't have to be a genius to do it. You just need to know a few basics, have a working plan and strategy, and be ready to stick to it.

Investing is the act of allocating funds or committing capital to an asset, like stocks, with the expectation of generating an income or profit. The expectation of a return in the form of income or price appreciation is the core premise of investing. Risk and return go hand-in-hand in investing; low risk generally means low expected returns, while higher returns are usually accompanied by higher risk.

One of the most common myths about investing is the idea that you need a lot of money to get started. Nothing could be further from the truth. If you can find £50 or $50 a month in your budget, you can and should start investing. If you think you can't squeeze that amount out of your budget, go and make it happen by cutting down your expenses and/or getting a part-time job. Now, if you carry high-interest debt or haven't set up your emergency account yet, you should attend to that first. But once you do, investing should be a priority on your list.

You don't need to know everything from day one to get started. Every successful investor I know starts with the basics, and many of them started small, building their wealth over time. No matter how much or little money you have, the important thing is to educate yourself on the basics of how you can get your money to work for you. And those basics are covered in this book.

At the end of the day, if you learn just the basics of investing, you are 90% on the way to investment success. Once you understand these basics, your fears of investing will decrease. That's not to say it will be smooth sailing every day, but you will be better equipped to keep things in perspective if you keep your focus on the long-term.

No one can guarantee that you'll make money from the investments you make. But if you get the facts about investing and follow through with a simple but smart plan, you should be able to gain financial security over the years. Investing is a marathon, not a sprint. Always think that you are in it for the long haul.

I often ask people to tell me their 'WHY' for investing? It is important to know the motivation behind your decision to invest your money. It's okay if you have many answers to this question, but there is a big problem if you have no answer at all. Don't invest because I'm telling you to do so. Don't invest because of peer pressure, don't invest because of FOMO (Fear Of Missing Out). Having clear reasons or purposes for investing is critical to investing successfully.

I usually wrap up my books by talking about the importance of financial education. If this book is the first book on investing you've ever read, don't let it be the last. Read more books about investing, keep learning, listen to podcasts, ask questions, attend financial literacy seminars, sign up for finance courses, seek knowledge, make learning a habit.

Even if it's something small, try learning at least one new thing about investing every day. Be mindful of your continuing education. Go into the day having a specific goal in mind, or an investing area in which you want to develop. By keeping in mind that you should always be learning, you'll easily continue your education and make strides toward the financial freedom and financial independence we all yearn for!

The Beauty of Compounding

ABOUT OYENIKE ADETOYE

Oyenike (also known as Nike) is an impactful speaker, author, and personal finance expert. A Chartered Management Accountant by profession, Nike founded LifTED Finance Consulting Ltd, a private financial firm that educates, coaches and supports people on their journey through financial fitness and wealth management.

Nike defines success by the number of lives impacted, changed and empowered through her message of hope in the area of personal finance. Her recent book series: "NonSecrets of the Financially Secure", "Praying for your Finances", "Financial Nakedness", and "Financially Smart Teens & Young Adults" provides simple guiding principles that empower people to win with their money. She is happily married and blessed with two beautiful children.

Connect with Oyenike online:
W▶ http://www.liftedfinance.com/
E▶ info@liftedfinance.com
T▶ https://twitter.com/FinanceLifted
F▶ https://www.facebook.com/liftedfinanceconsultingltd/
I ▶ https://www.instagram.com/liftedfinance/
L▶ https://www.linkedin.com/company/liftedfinanceconsulting/

The Beauty of Compounding

THE BEAUTY OF COMPOUNDING

By: Oyenike Adetoye   ACMA, CGMA

"When it comes to investing, nothing will pay off more than educating yourself. The most important thing you can do to be a successful investor is to learn, learn, learn and never stop learning."

- Oyenike Adetoye

Printed in Great Britain
by Amazon

41583935R00096